THE ORIGINS
OF THE ENGLISH CIVIL WAR

Conspiracy, Crusade, or Class Conflict?

PROBLEMS IN EUROPEAN CIVILIZATION

THE ORIGINS
OF THE
ENGLISH CIVIL WAR

Conspiracy, Crusade, or Class Conflict?

EDITED WITH AN INTRODUCTION BY

Philip A. M. Taylor

UNIVERSITY OF HULL, ENGLAND

D. C. HEATH AND COMPANY
A Division of Raytheon Education Company
Lexington, Massachusetts

Table of Contents

PART III: TEN VARIATIONS: SOME CONTRIBUTIONS
OF MODERN SCHOLARSHIP

Introduction

Most English people who are not professional students have had their view of the origins of the Civil War formed, directly or indirectly, by the first chapter of Macaulay's *History*. This is partly because, from the vantage point of modern constitutional history, the Parliamentarians in that conflict are seen to have been on the winning side. But the lasting popularity of Macaulay derives also from his forceful style and the sweeping confidence of his interpretations. He points out that James I and Charles I were far more extreme and outspoken in their claims than Elizabeth had been; yet there was no crisis of national peril to inhibit opposition. The natural enemy of royal claims, he thinks, was Puritanism inside and outside Parliament. When, in 1640, Charles was forced by financial difficulties to summon Parliament once more, its leaders, "great statesmen" as Macaulay terms them, at once devoted their energies to limiting his power. Increasingly distrustful of the king's intentions, Parliament refused him control of the armed forces needed to suppress rebellion in Ireland. Charles' retaliation, in attempting to arrest five members of the Commons, made inevitable a war to limit the royal prerogative. Macaulay is sure that it would have been better to depose the king, as was done in 1688; but he admits that no one in 1642 could face such a drastic course.

This "Whig interpretation" has prevailed among those interested chiefly in the growth of constitutional liberty. But, from quite a different point of view, Marxists have ascribed great importance to the Civil War which, to them, is a "bourgeois revolution," the political act by which English capitalism overthrew "feudal" society and insured for itself favorable conditions for development. Despite reissues in 1949 and 1955, Christopher Hill's *The English Revolution* is a youthful work by a man who has since written of the period in more complex and mature fashion. But it is a forceful presentation of the Marxist view, by one of the very few English historians who can use the contributions of Soviet scholars.[1] Hill rejects any interpretation of the origins of the Civil War which ascribes an independent role to individuals, to politics, or to religion. For Marxists, reality lies beneath all these, in the successive stages of productive organization and in the rise and fall of classes. The excerpt here printed shows the characteristic Marxist mingling of materialist interpretation and expressions of moral denunciation or praise; the obsession with what contributes to or opposes the "advance" of the historical process; and, it may be suggested, the willingness to employ, according to the situation which has to be explained, several logically distinct concepts of "class."

Although these two excerpts constitute perhaps the major contrasting interpretations of modern times, explanations of the origins of the Civil War did not arise only in the nineteenth and twentieth centuries. On the contrary, they began when the sounds of gunfire and of marching feet had scarcely died away. Among them, the one literary masterpiece is Clarendon's *History of the Great Rebellion*. Written nearly thirty years after the events described, the book contains errors due to tricks of memory, and an element of self-justification in its unwillingness to recognize how far the author, as a young Member, had voted with his colleagues in the near unanimity

[1] My own ignorance of Russian allows me to do no more than record Hill's opinion that the most thorough study of our subject ever made is that by E. A. Kosminsky and Y. A. Levitsky, 2 vols., Moscow, 1954, the English translation of whose title is *The English Bourgeois Revolution of the Seventeenth Century*.

of the Long Parliament's first months. He admits that Charles I was badly advised and made mistakes. But he is equally sure that the mass of moderate Members of Parliament were led astray by Pym, Holles, St. John, Vane, and, most formidable in his opinion, Hampden. These men he flatly accuses of aiming at rebellion. Later, as he describes, the moderates, under his own leadership, rallied to the defense of the essential rights of King and Church. In all this, Clarendon gives full weight to the effects of class interest in the development of the conflict. But he sees clearly that "economic interests cannot mobilize themselves," and so gives prominence to personalities, each "half an agent, half a victim, in the avalanche so imprudently set sliding."[2]

If Clarendon represents statesmanlike Royalism, Mrs. Hutchinson represents extreme Puritanism. In her biography of her husband, a prominent Parliamentarian who died in prison under Charles II, she sees priestcraft and tyranny inextricably mingled on the one side, true spiritual religion and the defense of legal rights on the other. To her, Puritans were people who wanted a truly religious Reformation, not the mere political change presided over by Henry VIII. To her, Charles I and his advisers seemed sympathetic toward Rome and watched with envy the growth of absolutism in Europe. Laud, Strafford, and above all Queen Henrietta Maria are singled out for special attack.

Thomas Hobbes' *Behemoth* differs greatly from his earlier and more famous book *Leviathan*, being more historical and less systematically philosophical. Yet both books reflect the tensions of the 1640's and 1650's and are the work of a man obsessed by society's need of authority and order to curb the violent and destructive passions of the human race. He has no sympathy for rebels and is entirely cynical about their religious professions. But his remarks on the divine character of monarchy do not give the impression of sincerity. Hobbes is interested in social factors among the origins of the Civil War. But, more than most commentators, he takes seriously the role of ideas. Where he stands apart is in his view that intellectual freedom produced evil rather than good.

Richard Baxter's autobiography was written later than the books just mentioned. He shows himself a more moderate Puritan than Mrs. Hutchinson: a cautious Presbyterian rather than a militant Independent. He recognizes the importance of social factors. He tends to identify Puritanism with the Parliamentary cause. He is aware of the changes of attitude that took place as events unfolded and distinguishes between the original disputes and the factors that caused men to fight fiercely on one side or the other once the war had begun. He deplores violence and arrogance on both sides, and feels that the later course of the rebellion reflected Cromwell's personal ambitions. Above all, in a fashion unique among his contemporaries, Baxter is willing to doubt his own judgment.

The remaining excerpts do not represent all the interpretations ever put forward about the origins of the Civil War. For example, only a long and complex narrative could fully illustrate the view hinted at by Bulstrode Whitelocke in 1642, when he said that Parliament "insensibly slipped into the beginning of a civil war by one unexpected accident after another."[3] The nearest approximation to this view in modern times, the chapter entitled "The Drift to War" in J. W. Allen's *English Political Thought 1603–1660*, was reluctantly omitted. Yet another view, not defended by any professional historian, has been argued passionately and at length in the books of Esmé Wingfield-Stratford noted in *Suggestions for Additional Reading*. He asserts that Charles I was in the main the innocent victim of a faction, led by Pym, which was hostile to his benevolent paternalism, and which consciously and con-

[2] Both phrases are from Trevor-Roper, *Historical Essays,* p. 247.

[3] Quoted Hexter, *The Reign of King Pym,* p. 8.

sistently used the foulest means to discredit and entrap him. Even if this central thesis is found unacceptable, Wingfield-Stratford's work has the merit of emphasizing the element of violence, in the years 1641 and 1642, so often glossed over by the Whigs. We are studying not a constitutional debate, but a revolution: though what kind of revolution remains open to argument.

As the reader studies the excerpts from these works, which present a broad or overall interpretation of the events leading up to the outbreak of the Civil War, he will undoubtedly become aware that each of these broad or general viewpoints is the product of a great number of subsidiary interpretations of each of the separate events which in their conjunctive force produced the final conflict. Each of these, therefore, must be examined in detail if one is to assess the validity of the broader interpretive view. For example, is it true that Charles I aimed at tyranny and repeatedly broke faith with the English people? Was the Grand Remonstrance of 1641 accurate in its catalogue of government misdeeds and oppression — which ranged from the imprisonment of Members of Parliament, the intimidation of judges and the selling of titles, to "the desperate design of engrossing all the gunpowder into one hand, keeping it in the Tower of London"? What *was* the character of Charles' rule? On the other hand, what were the real aims of the House of Commons; and were they fairly consistent, or did they shift significantly as events unfolded? What was that "Constitution" to which Macaulay refers so often as a standard of judgment? To what extent are the origins of the Civil War to be found in the personal rule of Charles I, in the policies of his father, or in even earlier developments? How does it come about that the Grand Remonstrance embodies a general theory of the existence of a "malignant party," author of all wrongs, and linked with an international movement "composed, set up, and acted by the subtile practice of the Jesuites and other engineers

and factors for Rome"? How much weight is to be given to the fact that men so often spoke in religious terms? Was the conflict of 1642 "inevitable," and if so from what date? Could changes in policy or more skillful management have averted war, or were the political struggles, the manoeuvres of individuals, even the religious policies shaped by underlying social forces — waves upon which Charles and Pym, Laud and Vane, Strafford and Hampden merely floated? About such questions able historians of our own time fiercely disagree. The ten excerpts in Part III are a sample of these modern views. They do not cover all the possible interpretations. Nor do they necessarily answer or contradict each other in any neat and direct fashion. But, in addition to the merits of their own reasoning, several of them have the advantage of summarizing, or presenting in quotation, characteristic seventeenth-century ideas. They have been selected, it must be emphasized, in such a way as to deal with developments up to 1642. After that date, with open fighting, a new era began: some institutions crumbled, alignments changed, and many novel ideas were advanced.

The first three of these excerpts are concerned with interpretations of the Civil War in terms of class interests. The central controversy here is about the part played by that class rather vaguely called the Gentry. In 1941 the distinguished economic historian, R. H. Tawney, in a now famous article entitled "The Rise of the Gentry," suggested that in a period of rising prices, and of great transfers of land because of the economic squeeze on the old aristocracy, a decisive economic advantage was gained by the gentry — most of whom regarded farming as a business — who acquired land on favorable terms, while both the small men who lacked resources and the aristocracy with their antiquated methods and lavish display lost ground. Because the Crown too had lost much of its economic power, the Civil War could be provoked and carried to a successful conclusion by the gentry, who aimed in this way to bring their political influence into line with their economic power.

The elaboration of this thesis of the decline of the aristocracy by Lawrence Stone, in his article dealing with that class under Elizabeth, provoked a violent attack ·by H. R. Trevor-Roper, which developed into a series of articles attacking all Tawney's propositions. The line of attack varies from one article to another. One shows the weakness of Stone's or Tawney's statistics. Another emphasizes the strong propensity to rebellion among the poorer rather than the more powerful gentry. Yet another analyzes the conflict of the 1620's between the Court and a group of M.P.'s, who were elder statesmen by 1640, and who were overthrown, in turn, by their more radical allies, the lesser gentry. Throughout, however, Trevor-Roper insists on the need to distinguish between men who held lucrative royal offices and those whose income was derived solely from land. The latter, he asserts, were declining, not rising, and so were ripe for revolt, though their aims were wholly destructive.

J. H. Hexter's recent article in *Encounter* attacks both sides in this controversy, although he sees some value in certain of Trevor-Roper's arguments. Hexter thinks Tawney's statistics misleading, but suggests that the judgments of contemporaries were not necessarily more reliable. He denies that the gentry and aristocracy were distinct economic groups; and he argues that the most important group throughout the period were the prosperous gentry who dominated the House of Commons, but who, nevertheless, had interests in common with other classes as well as ambitions of their own. His conclusion is that until very late these men aimed at regulating royal power rather than at seizing supremacy for themselves. Finally he insists on the importance of their political and religious principles, which he thinks they placed above the mere pursuit of special interests.

By the time he has reached this point, it will probably be apparent to the reader that his studies are greatly complicated by the fact that the disputants are not always asking exactly the same questions. Some are interested in the total development of England, or of English capitalism. Some are concerned to explain the forces which later brought Cromwell into prominence. Some are interested above all in the years 1640–1642. The result, as a full reading of their articles will show, is that these scholars often miss certain aspects of their opponents' arguments, and drastically simplify their antagonists' conclusions in order to make their own point about a slightly different sector of the subject. The plain fact is that, since the gentry were the only large class politically articulate in the early seventeenth century, some of them will be found at the head of *every* movement.

Whatever the class interests involved, men spoke largely in religious terms; and even if the expression "Puritan Revolution" has gone out of fashion, Puritanism must be examined closely. The separate items in the Puritan program are familiar enough: the emphasis on preaching and extemporary prayer as against formal liturgy; the dislike of wearing the surplice or of kneeling to receive Communion; the dislike of ornament in churches and of music in services, by which, as one preacher put it, "the sacrament is turned wel neere into a theatricall stage play"[4]; and finally, the opposition to the enforcement of ceremonial practices by bishops and courts. It is clear enough that the changes in tone within the Church's leadership in the early seventeenth century intensified Puritan distrust and resentment. Because the Church of England was closely interwoven with the entire social order as a holder of property and jurisdictional rights, and in a variety of ways aided the government, these grievances cannot be regarded as wholly ecclesiastical, still less as purely spiritual. But for all their validity, such familiar statements make of Puritanism only a negative force. It is the merit of Professor Haller that in all his books he points up the positive ideals of Puritanism:

[4] Quoted Mathew, *The Social Structure in Caroline England,* pp. 79–80 note.

its code of life and its sense of dedication to active service in the world. He shows how its adherents saw themselves as clearly distinguishable from people with less exacting standards; and he suggests that as a result they were bound to feel that worldly social rank was relatively unimportant, as compared to the essential equality of the elect and their inherent superiority over the unregenerate.

For all their merits, Haller's views are open to two critical comments. In the first place, he usually discusses Puritanism in its noblest aspects. But it also possessed far uglier elements, which became prominent in moments of crisis: the bitterness and injustice of its polemics; Pym's twisted "editing" of Laud's diary for publication; the incessant demands for the persecution of Roman Catholics and even for the execution of individual priests; the Covenanters' battle-cry at Tibbermore, "Jesus and no quarter"; the killing of prisoners after the battle of Philiphaugh, and of women camp-followers, assumed to be Irish Catholics, after Naseby. Secondly, while one may grant the power of Puritanism over men's minds, Haller fails to make clear precisely whither it led them in the organization of their power, especially in the political field. An interesting beginning to the study of this subject was made by Hexter in his book on John Pym. In this he is concerned primarily with the years of Pym's supremacy, 1642–1643; but in the selection from it here printed he shows the close association between men who later became leading Puritan Parliamentarians. They were associated first in a variety of colonizing enterprises undertaken to provide havens for Puritan refugees, and second in resistance to the famous ship-money levies. In a passage here omitted, he goes on to show how commonly they intermarried to form family "connexions" — in which the Earls of Bedford, Lincoln and Warwick were especially prominent — which helped to strengthen the Puritan hand politically.

Turning from religious to political factors, the "Whig interpretation" of the events of the early seventeenth century has always depended heavily on the arguments, first, that Charles was a tyrant, aiming quite consciously at the subversion of established rights, and second, that there existed a "constitution" which the Stuarts persistently violated. Much of the work of modern scholars has been focused on these two related topics.

D. H. Willson, for example, describes the reduced power of the royal Council during the first three decades of the century as a result of James' policy of using it as an instrument of patronage rather than government. Whereas, by effective use of a Council made up of the wisest and ablest men available, Elizabeth had exercised great influence over Parliament, James I and Charles I appointed mediocrities or men who, however able as bureaucrats, carried no weight in the House of Commons. Hence a crucial instrument of royal authority was allowed to become blunted. Miss Wedgwood, in a chapter in the first volume of several which she plans to write on the history of the Great Rebellion, likewise reveals the weaknesses and dissensions within Charles I's personal government of the 1630's. She suggests that even if the King's aim was despotism, he was incapable of willing the means necessary to achieve it.

As for the "constitution," one prominent scholar in the field of English Constitutional History, Miss Margaret Judson, has taken pains to show the lack of any clear understanding or precise definition of such a "constitution" among the men on either side. By citing the habitual forms of utterance of ordinary Members of Parliament, or lawyers, rather than the formal statements or theoretical speculations of a few outstanding and forward-looking minds, she tries to depict as accurately as possible the climate of opinion in the first decades of the seventeenth century. She concludes that most men held that there existed a balanced constitution which at one and the same time guaranteed ample powers for the king and security for the rights of subjects.

She shows that both sides appealed — and in a sense correctly — to law and precedent. But constitutional theories are, after all, no more than the framework within which practical policies and practical grievances are discussed; and the theory of a balanced constitution tended to break down as soon as a government seemed to be unworthy of trust, and to be intent upon its own aggrandisement. In their disputes over what many judged to be legitimate grievances, Miss Judson thinks, Englishmen found it necessary to elaborate their arguments in such a way as to encroach, from both sides, upon an area in which, before 1603, no constitutional definitions had been attempted. Even so, she insists, arguments as to whether "sovereignty" resided in King or Parliament did not arise in any clear-cut fashion until fighting had started.

If, looked at from the distance of three centuries, the theories of most men seem to have been moderate and even confused, their actions reveal obstinacy, bad temper, suspicion, and fear, and it is important to understand how far such manifestations of human irascibility — and human miscalculation too — contributed to the final crisis. Such matters receive very full treatment in the second selection from Miss Wedgwood. In a detailed and perceptive account of the events of the last weeks of 1641 and the first of 1642 she shows how, as the crisis approached and tension heightened, emotion came to supplant reason. For emotional appeals were more effective in arousing that mass support which would be needed if the controversy was to be determined by force. Similarly tactics changed, as each side became more concerned to discredit its opponents than to convince them.

Miss Wedgwood declares that she has tried to tell her story "in such a way as to bring out the hourly urgency and confusion through which contemporaries lived." So logically does this story move — from move to counter-move, from charge to counter-charge, with each step becoming more extreme — that one may too hastily conclude that here at last is a sound basis for arriving at an understanding of the origins of the Civil War. Yet, as Miss Wedgwood herself recognizes, this is only one "level" of study. Other scholars may, quite as legitimately, study "underlying forces." Similarly, since in politics personalities are always significant, and in the seventeenth century perhaps even more significant than today, other scholars again may try to estimate the abilities, character, and principles of kings, ministers, politicians, bishops. This is one of the things that Ranke tried to do (and has anyone bettered his portrait of Charles I?); and, at a different level, Wingfield-Stratford employs pseudo-psychoanalytical methods to explain the personality and motives of Charles on the basis of his physical disabilities and childhood experiences.

As one studies the selections presented in this pamphlet, and still more as one scans the extensive list of titles given at the end, it may seem that the origins of the Civil War have been so exhaustively studied by scholars that only a few minor aspects can remain to be investigated. In fact, however, each generation seeks to understand its past in terms which are meaningful within the framework of its own ideas; and an interpretation which has satisfied one generation, as answering those questions in which it is most interested, seems quite inadequate to the next. For the nineteenth century, so proud of the triumph of parliamentary government, political factors seemed to provide the key to understanding the Civil War. In the early decades of the twentieth century, social and economic factors seemed crucial. In mid-twentieth century, with its revival of interest in religion and in secular "isms," interest in the ideological aspect of the Puritan Revolution has revived. In the final selection, Christopher Hill, who in an earlier excerpt presented the Marxist interpretation of the problem, makes an interesting and provocative survey of those aspects which to him, a professional historian writing in the 1950's, seem to need further research and reflection. The student should find it both interesting and useful to consider how far he would agree with Hill's judgments.

Although the reader will undoubtedly recognize and accept without second thought the need to break down the broad general problem of Civil War origins into many component parts for purposes of analysis, he must resist the tendency to separate these so radically as to lost sight of the "forest" in concentrating too much on individual "trees." The separate institutions that must be studied were closely linked: Church and property; Church and law courts; bishops and kings; Parliament and law; property and other rights of the subject. Any attack on, or desire to change, one institution was likely to involve others.

Furthermore, as the conflict developed, the men involved came to develop ideologies, systems of thought by which they tried to give consistency to their varied immediate objectives, and coherence to their varied hopes and fears. Such a mental process often led to the linking together, in an arbitrary and misleading fashion, of quite distinct and unrelated events.

Charles I, for example, when thwarted in particular aims, came to feel that he was faced with a broad challenge to what he felt was his ancient and lawful authority. Pique and frustration made him easily susceptible to the view that if he surrendered even the tiniest portion of that authority, he would be betraying his responsibility to God and to his own posterity. At the same time, a Puritan was bound to seem to him not only a disturber of religious order but, given the character of the Church of England, equally an enemy of God-given authority in the state.

A Puritan Member of Parliament was likely to have an even more unified worldview, in an age that saw the Thirty Years' War in Europe, as well as the origins of civil war in England. He linked Arminianism with Popery, and both with absolutism. He linked the peace policy of James I, or conversions to Rome among Charles I's courtiers, with a European movement hostile to Protestantism and liberty alike. He looked back to the age of Elizabeth and thought he saw there a consistent anti-Catholic and anti-Spanish policy: as Ranke put it, in 1621 "Parliament demanded the policy of Queen Elizabeth; King James demanded her rights."[5] Parliament continually demanded a more active foreign policy in what was conceived to be an international Protestant interest; for, as Sir Edwin Sandys put it, "our religion is rooted out in Bohemia and Germany, and rooting out in France." The Roman Catholic counterattack was linked in men's minds with Spain. "The designes of Spain," said Sir Robert Phelips in 1621, "are ever accompanied by falsehood, being resting on that great Roman monster," while Sir Edward Coke blamed Spain for everything from the Gunpowder Plot to the introduction into Europe of syphilis.[6] Such was the frame of reference into which grievances, fears, ambitions, and rumors were fitted.

At the age of sixteen, James, then king only in Scotland, was told by his tutor, George Buchanan, "At this early age, you have pursued the history of almost every nation and have committed many of them to memory."[7] Something more than that is demanded of the student of history today; for, as this collection of readings shows, scholars differ widely, not merely about the history of a nation, but about one great episode within it. Even the highly condensed list of suggestions for further reading at the end of this pamphlet contains something like one hundred titles. Yet much remains to be done before our understanding is complete — if, indeed, it can ever be complete. At best, the editor can hope to have done no more than indicate to the student what leading scholars judge to be the principal issues, present samples of the main lines of argument, and hint at the topics on which further research is needed.

[5] Ranke, *History of England* . . . , Vol. I, p. 508.
[6] The quotations appear in Brett, *Pym*, p. 37; Mathew, *The Jacobean Age*, p. 191; Bowen, *The Lion and the Throne*, pp. 387–8.
[7] Quoted Willson, *King James VI and I*, p. 23.

A NOTE ON SEVENTEENTH–CENTURY LANGUAGE

While reading the first four excerpts, and some of the quotations embodied in others, the student should understand that some words were commonly used in a different sense from what is customary today. Among them are the following:

Country	often means County
Intelligence	usually means News
Lecturer	a preacher not in charge of a parish, but appointed by town council or gentry to preach, usually Puritan sermons, without necessarily reading the Common Prayer services
Parts	Abilities
Pretend	Claim
Sort	often means Rank
Treaty	usually a Negotiation, not the document which concludes it
Wanted	usually Lacked

There are many variations in the spelling of seventeenth-century proper names, e.g. Abbot, Haslerig, Holles; but it is unlikely that these will cause confusion.

The Conflict of Opinion

Many English Kings had occasionally committed unconstitutional acts: but none had ever systematically attempted to make himself a despot, and to reduce Parliament to a nullity. Such was the end which Charles distinctly proposed to himself.

— THOMAS B. MACAULAY

Queen Elizabeth . . . had been respected and feared, but she had also been popular, and she had never allowed any crisis to arise in which her power was pitted against the will of her justices or her people. King Charles had too high an opinion of the Crown's authority to consider the necessity of maintaining the equilibrium. . . . The council became the heart and centre of Court intrigues rather than the heart and centre of government. . . . The king was serious-minded, but he was not industrious. . . . His casual attitude to his council, his unwillingness to listen to disturbing information, his hunting three or four times a week, the long hours spent in pursuit or enjoyment of works of art, or in theological discussion — all tell the same tale. He was not interested in practical administration. He idled away the opportunities of his reign.

— C. V. WEDGWOOD

The causes of the civil war must be sought in society, not in individuals. . . . A victory for Charles I and his gang could only have meant the economic stagnation of England, the stabilisation of a backward feudal society in a commercial age. . . . The Parliamentarians thought they were fighting God's battles. They were certainly fighting those of posterity, throwing off an intolerable incubus to further advance.

— CHRISTOPHER HILL

The ruin of famous families by personal extravagance and political ineptitude; the decline of the position of the yeomanry . . . ; the loss, not only of revenue, but of authority, by the monarchy, as Crown lands melted; the mounting of fortunes of the residuary legatee, the gentry . . . who steadily gathered into their hands estates slipping from the grasp of peasant, nobility, Church and Crown alike — such movements were visible to all. . . . A shrewd foreigner remarked . . . that the Stuarts were on the way to be overshadowed in wealth by their subjects before they were overthrown by them.

— RICHARD H. TAWNEY

The Great Rebellion . . . is not the clear-headed self-assertion of the rising bourgeoisie and gentry, but rather the blind protest of the depressed gentry, . . . the blind revolt of the gentry against the Court, of the provinces against the capital: the backwash against a century of administrative and economic centralisation . . . a protest, by the victims of a temporary general depression, against a privileged bureaucracy, a capitalist City.

— HUGH R. TREVOR-ROPER

Each class created and sought to impose the religious outlook best suited to its own needs and interests. But the real clash is between these class interests.

— CHRISTOPHER HILL

The Puritan code was much more than a table of prohibitions. It was the program of an active, not a monastic or contemplative, life. . . . When God called his elect to repent and believe, he also called upon them to act. The gifts and opportunities . . . with which the saint was invested were also part of his commission from God. Whatsoever we undertake in the exercise of our talents and in the spirit of faith is good. It is what God has called us to do.

— WILLIAM HALLER

The active Puritan groups remind us of nothing so much as a *congeries* of independent corporations with directorates conveniently interlocking . . . from another angle . . . a family party.

— J. H. HEXTER

It seemed, therefore [1625], that the decisive hour was approaching, and that the English Parliament would soon either share the fate of the senates of the Continent, or obtain supreme ascendancy in the state.

— THOMAS B. MACAULAY

The ideal of balance was one of the most cherished and strongest beliefs Englishmen agreed upon between 1603 and 1640. . . . To believe in both the divine right of kingly authority and at the same time in its limited nature was perfectly natural and consistent for many excellent seventeenth-century minds. . . . Until 1628 most Englishmen, including the leaders of the parliamentary opposition, seem to have believed that the king's discretionary power to act for the general welfare was both legal and necessary. . . . As kings possessed prerogatives, so subjects possessed rights; and these rights, like the king's prerogatives, were part of the law and basic in the constitution. The most important of these rights were property rights.

— MARGARET A. JUDSON

From the accession of Elizabeth I to the summoning of the Long Parliament the rich country gentlemen who fill the House of Commons make no consistent or concerted effort to win permanent control or direction of the government.

— J. H. HEXTER

PART I: TWO THEMES: POLITICS AND ECONOMICS IN THE ORIGINS OF THE CIVIL WAR

Liberty Versus Despotism: The Classic Whig Statement

THOMAS BABINGTON MACAULAY

Macaulay (1800–59) had a career in public service as well as in letters. After education at private schools and Trinity College, Cambridge, he was called to the Bar in 1826, a year after he had published his first *Edinburgh Review* essay. Member of Parliament in 1830, he went to India four years later as a member of the Supreme Council. There, until 1837, he took a leading part in preparing the Criminal Code, as well as the plan for the higher education of Indians through English rather than local languages. Later he was Secretary at War, Paymaster General, and refused a third high office in order to complete his *History,* the first instalment of which appeared in 1848. Retiring from the House of Commons, Macaulay was raised to the peerage in 1857. The excerpt is taken from the first of three introductory chapters, before the main narrative of the *History* begins.

OF James the First, as of John, it may be said that, if his administration had been able and splendid, it would probably have been fatal to our country, and that we owe more to his weakness and meanness than to the wisdom and courage of much better sovereigns. He came to the throne at a critical moment. The time was fast approaching when either the King must become absolute, or the Parliament must control the whole executive administration. Had James been, like Henry the Fourth, like Maurice of Nassau, or like Gustavus Adolphus, a valiant, active, and politic ruler, had he put himself at the head of the Protestants of Europe, had he gained great victories over Tilly and Spinola, had he adorned Westminster with the spoils of Bavarian monasteries and Flemish cathedrals, had he hung Austrian and Castilian banners in St. Paul's, and had he found himself, after great achievements, at the head of fifty thousand troops, brave, well disciplined, and devotedly attached to his person, the English Parliament would soon have been nothing more than a name. Happily he was not a man to play such a part. He began his administration by putting an end to the war which had raged during many years between England and Spain; and from that time he shunned hostilities with a caution which was proof against the insults of his neighbours and the clamours of his subjects. Not till the last year of his

From *The History of England from the Accession of James II* (1848–61), Volume I, by Baron Thomas Babington Macaulay. Everyman's Library. Reprinted by permission of J. M. Dent and E. P. Dutton & Co., Inc., pp. 52–3, 55–6, 57–8, 62–9, 73, 76–9, 81–4.

1

life could the influence of his son, his favourite, his Parliament and his people combined, induce him to strike one feeble blow in defence of his family and of his religion. It was well for those whom he governed, that he in this matter disregarded their wishes. The effect of his pacific policy was that, in his time, no regular troops were needed, and that, while France, Spain, Italy, Belgium, and Germany swarmed with mercenary soldiers, the defence of our island was still confided to the militia.

As the King had no standing army, and did not even attempt to form one, it would have been wise in him to avoid any conflict with his people. But such was his indiscretion that, while he altogether neglected the means which alone could make him really absolute, he constantly put forward, in the most offensive form, claims of which none of his predecessors had ever dreamed. It was at this time that those strange theories which Filmer afterwards formed into a system, and which became the badge of the most violent class of Tories and high churchmen, first emerged into notice. It was gravely maintained that the Supreme Being regarded hereditary monarchy, as opposed to other forms of government, with peculiar favour; that the rule of succession in order of primogeniture was a divine institution, anterior to the Christian, and even to the Mosaic dispensation; that no human power, not even that of the whole legislature, no length of adverse possession, though it extended to ten centuries, could deprive the legitimate prince of his rights; that his authority was necessarily always despotic; that the laws by which, in England and in other countries, the prerogative was limited were to be regarded merely as concessions which the sovereign had freely made and might at his pleasure resume; and that any treaty into which a king might enter with his people was merely a declaration of his present intentions, and not a contract of which the performance could be demanded.

Thus, at the very moment at which a republican spirit began to manifest itself strongly in the Parliament and in the country, the claims of the monarch took a monstrous form which would have disgusted the proudest and most arbitrary of those who had preceded him on the throne.

James was always boasting of his skill in what he called kingcraft; and yet it is hardly possible even to imagine a course more directly opposed to all the rules of kingcraft than that which he followed. The policy of wise rulers has always been to disguise strong acts under popular forms. It was thus that Augustus and Napoleon established absolute monarchies, while the public regarded them merely as eminent citizens invested with temporary magistracies. The policy of James was the direct reverse of theirs. He enraged and alarmed his Parliament by constantly telling them that they held their privileges merely during his pleasure, and that they had no more business to inquire what he might lawfully do than what the Deity might lawfully do. Yet he quailed before them, abandoned minister after minister to their vengeance, and suffered them to tease him into acts directly opposed to his strongest inclinations. Thus the indignation excited by his claims and the scorn excited by his concessions went on growing together. By his fondness for worthless minions, and by the sanction which he gave to their tyranny and rapacity, he kept discontent constantly alive. His cowardice, his childishness, his pedantry, his ungainly person and manners, his provincial accent made him an object of derision. Even in his virtues and accomplishments there was something eminently unkingly. Throughout the whole course of his reign, all the venerable associations by which the throne had long been fenced were gradually losing their strength. During two hundred years, all the sovereigns who had ruled England, with the single exception of the unfortunate Henry the Sixth, had been strongminded, high-spirited, courageous, and of princely bearing. Almost all had possessed abilities above the ordinary level. It was no light thing that, on the very eve of the decisive struggle between our Kings and their Parliaments, royalty should be exhibited to the world stammering, slobbering, shedding unmanly tears, trembling at a drawn sword, and talking in the style alternately of a buffoon and of a pedagogue.

In the meantime the religious dissensions, by which, from the days of Edward the Sixth, the Protestant body had been distracted, had become more formidable than ever.

The founders of the Anglican Church had retained episcopacy as an ancient, a decent, and a convenient ecclesiastical polity, but had not declared that form of church government to be of divine institution. In the reign of Elizabeth, Jewel, Cooper, Whitgift, and other eminent doctors defended prelacy as innocent, as useful, as what the state might lawfully establish, as what, when established by the state, was entitled to the respect of every citizen. But they never denied that a Christian community without a Bishop might be a pure Church. On the contrary, they regarded the Protestants of the Continent as of the same household of faith with themselves. Englishmen in England were indeed bound to acknowledge the authority of the Bishop, as they were bound to acknowledge the authority of the Sheriff and of the Coroner: but the obligation was purely local. An English churchman, nay even an English prelate, if he went to Holland, conformed without scruple to the established religion of Holland. Abroad the ambassadors of Elizabeth and James went in state to the very worship which Elizabeth and James persecuted at home, and carefully abstained from decorating their private chapels after the Anglican fashion, lest scandal should be given to weaker brethren. In the year 1603, the Convocation of the province of Canterbury solemnly recognised the Church of Scotland, a Church in which episcopal control and episcopal ordination were then unknown, as a branch of the Holy Catholic Church of Christ. It was even held that Presbyterian ministers were entitled to

place and voice in oecumenical councils. When the States General of the United Provinces convoked at Dort a synod of doctors not episcopally ordained, an English Bishop and an English Dean, commissioned by the head of the English Church, sat with these doctors, preached to them, and voted with them on the gravest questions of theology. Nay, many English benefices were held by divines who had been admitted to the ministry in the Calvinistic form used on the Continent; nor was reordination by a Bishop in such cases thought necessary, or even lawful.

But a new race of divines was already rising in the Church of England. In their view the episcopal office was essential to the welfare of a Christian society and to the efficacy of the most solemn ordinances of religion. To that office belonged certain high and sacred privileges, which no human power could give or take away. A church might as well be without the doctrine of the Trinity, or the doctrine of the Incarnation, as without the apostolical orders; and the Church of Rome, which, in the midst of all her corruptions, had retained the apostolical orders, was nearer to primitive purity than those reformed societies which had rashly set up, in opposition to the divine model, a system invented by men.

In the days of Edward the Sixth and of Elizabeth, the defenders of the Anglican ritual had generally contented themselves with saying that it might be used without sin, and that, therefore, none but a perverse and undutiful subject would refuse to use it when enjoined to do so by the magistrate. Now, however, that rising party which claimed for the polity of the Church a celestial origin began to ascribe to her services a new dignity and importance. It was hinted that, if the established worship had any fault, that fault was extreme simplicity, and that the Reformers had, in the heat of their quarrel with Rome, abolished many ancient ceremonies which might with advantage have been retained. Days and places were again held in mysterious veneration. Some practices which had long been disused, and which were commonly regarded as superstitious mummeries, were revived. Paintings and carvings, which had escaped the fury of the first generation of Protestants, became the objects of a respect such as to many seemed idolatrous.

Thus the political and religious schism which had originated in the sixteenth century was, during the first quarter of the seventeenth century, constantly widening. Theories tending to Turkish despotism were in fashion at Whitehall. Theories tending to republicanism were in favour with a large portion of the House of Commons. The violent Prelatists who were, to a man, zealous for the prerogative, and the violent Puritans who were, to a man, zealous for the privileges of Parliament, regarded each other with animosity more intense than that which, in the preceding generation, had existed between Catholics and Protestants.

While the minds of men were in this state, the country, after a peace of many years, at length engaged in a war which required strenuous exertions. This war hastened the approach of the great constitutional crisis. It was necessary that the King should have a large military force. He could not have such a force without money. He could not legally raise money without the consent of Parliament. It followed, therefore, that he must either administer the government in conformity with the sense of the House of Commons, or must venture on such a violation of the fundamental laws of the land as had been unknown during several centuries. The Plantagenets and Tudors had, it is true, occasionally supplied a deficiency in their revenue by a benevolence or a forced loan: but these expedients were always of a temporary nature. To meet the regular charge of a long war by regular taxation, imposed without the consent of the Estates of the realm, was a course which Henry the Eighth himself would not have dared to take. It seemed, therefore, that the decisive hour was approaching, and that the English Parliament would soon either share the fate of the senates of the Continent, or obtain supreme ascendancy in the state.

Just at this conjuncture James died. Charles the First succeeded to the throne. He had received from nature a far better understanding, a far stronger will, and a far keener and firmer temper than his father's. He had inherited his father's political theories, and was much more disposed than his father to carry them into practice. He was, like his father, a zealous episcopalian. He was, moreover, what his father had never been, a zealous Arminian, and, though no Papist, liked a Papist much better than a Puritan. It would be unjust to deny that Charles had some of the qualities of a good, and even of a great prince. He wrote and spoke, not, like his father, with the exactness of a professor, but after the fashion of intelligent and well educated gentlemen. His taste in literature and art was excellent, his manner dignified though not gracious, his domestic life without blemish. Faithlessness was the chief cause of his disasters, and is the chief stain on his memory. He was, in truth, impelled by an incurable propensity to dark and crooked ways. It may seem strange that his conscience, which, on occasions of little moment, was sufficiently sensitive, should never have reproached him with this great vice. But there is reason to believe that he was perfidious, not only from constitution and from habit, but also on principle. He seems to have learned from the theologians whom he most esteemed that between him and his subjects there could be nothing of the nature of mutual contract; that he could not, even if he would, divest himself of his despotic authority; and that, in every promise which he made, there was an implied reservation that such promise might be broken in case of necessity, and that of the necessity he was the sole judge.

And now began that hazardous game on which were staked the destinies of the English people. It was played on the side of the House of Commons with keenness, but with admirable dexterity, coolness, and perseverance. Great statesmen who looked far behind them and far before them were at the head of that assembly. They were resolved to place the King in such a situation that he must either conduct the administration in conformity with the wishes of his Parliament, or make outrageous attacks on the most sacred principles of the constitution. They accordingly doled out supplies to him very sparingly. He found that he must govern either in harmony with the House of Commons, or in defiance of all law. His choice was soon made. He dissolved his first Parliament, and levied taxes by his own authority. He convoked a second Parliament, and found it more intractable than the first. He again resorted to the expedient of dissolution, raised fresh taxes without any show of legal right, and threw the chiefs of the opposition into prison. At the same time a new grievance, which the peculiar feelings and habits of the English nation made insupportably painful, and which seemed to all discerning men to be of fearful augury, excited general discontent and alarm. Companies of soldiers were billeted on the people; and martial law was, in some places, substituted for the ancient jurisprudence of the realm.

The King called a third Parliament, and soon perceived that the opposition was stronger and fiercer than ever. He now determined on a change of tactics. Instead of opposing an inflexible resistance to the demands of the Commons, he, after much altercation and many evasions, agreed to a compromise which, if he had faithfully adhered to it, would have averted a long series of calamities. The Parliament granted an ample supply. The King ratified, in the most solemn manner, that celebrated law, which is known by the name of the Petition of Right, and which is the second Great Charter of the liberties of England. By ratifying that law he bound himself never again to raise money without the consent of the Houses, never again to imprison any person, except in due course of law, and never again to subject his people to the jurisdiction of courts martial.

The day on which the royal sanction was, after many delays, solemnly given to this great act, was a day of joy and hope. The Commons, who crowded to the bar of the House of Lords, broke forth into loud acclamations as soon as the clerk had pronounced the ancient form of words by which our princes have, during many ages, signified their assent to the wishes of the Estates of the realm. Those acclamations were reechoed by the voice of the capital and of the nation; but within three weeks it became manifest that Charles had no intention of observing the compact into which he had entered. The supply given by the representatives of the nation was collected. The promise by which that supply had been obtained was broken. A violent contest followed. The Parliament was dissolved with every mark of royal displeasure. Some of the most distinguished members were imprisoned; and one of them, Sir John Eliot, after years of suffering, died in confinement.

Charles, however, could not venture to raise, by his own authority, taxes sufficient for carrying on war. He accordingly hastened to make peace with his neighbours, and thenceforth gave his whole mind to British politics.

Now commenced a new era. Many English Kings had occasionally committed unconstitutional acts: but none had ever systematically attempted to make himself a despot, and to reduce Parliament to a nullity. Such was the end which Charles distinctly proposed to himself. From March 1629 to April 1640 the Houses were not convoked. Never in our history had there been an interval of eleven years between Parliament and Parliament. Only once had there been an interval of even half that length. This fact alone is sufficient to refute those who represent Charles as having merely trodden in the footsteps of the Plantagenets and Tudors.

It is proved, by the testimony of the King's most strenuous supporters, that, during this part of his reign, the provisions of the Petition of Right were violated by him, not occasionally, but constantly, and on system; that a large part of the revenue was raised without any legal authority; and that persons obnoxious to the government languished for years in prison, without being ever called upon to plead before any tribunal.

For these things history must hold the King himself chiefly responsible. From the time of his third Parliament he was his own prime minister. Several persons, however, whose temper and talents were suited to his purposes, were at the head of different departments of the administration.

Thomas Wentworth, successively created Lord Wentworth and Earl of Strafford, a man of great abilities, eloquence, and courage, but of a cruel and imperious nature, was the counsellor most trusted in political and military affairs. . . . His object was to do in England all, and more than all, that Richelieu was doing in France; to make Charles a monarch as absolute as any on the Continent; to put the estates and the personal liberty of the whole people at the disposal of the Crown; to deprive the courts of law of all independent authority, even in ordinary questions of civil right between man and man; and to punish with merciless rigour all who murmured at the acts of the government, or who applied, even in the most decent and regular manner, to any tribunal for relief against those acts.

. . . He saw that there was one instrument, and only one, by which his vast and daring projects could be carried into execution. That instrument was a standing army. To the forming of such an army, therefore, he directed all the energy of his strong mind. In Ireland, where he was viceroy, he actually succeeded in establishing a military despotism, not only over the aboriginal population, but also over the English colonists, and was able to boast that, in that island, the King was as absolute as any prince in the whole world could be.

The ecclesiastical administration was, in the meantime, principally directed by William Laud, Archbishop of Canterbury. Of all the prelates of the Anglican Church, Laud had departed farthest from the principles of the Reformation, and had drawn nearest to Rome. His theology was more remote than even that of the Dutch Arminians from the theology of the Calvinists. His passion for ceremonies, his reverence for holidays, vigils, and sacred places, his ill-concealed dislike of the marriage of ecclesiastics, the ardent and not altogether disinterested zeal with which he asserted the claims of the clergy to the reverence of the laity, would have made him an object of aversion to the Puritans, even if he had used only legal and gentle means for the attainment of his ends. But his understanding was narrow, and his commerce with the world had been small. He was by nature rash, irritable, quick to feel for his own dignity, slow to sympathize with the sufferings of others, and prone to the error, common in superstitious men, of mistaking his own peevish and malignant moods for emotions of pious zeal. Under his direction every corner of the realm was subjected to a constant and minute inspection. Every little congregation of separatists was tracked out and broken up. Even the devotions of private families could not escape the vigilance of his spies. Such fear did his rigour inspire that the deadly hatred of the Church, which festered in innumerable bosoms, was generally disguised under an outward show of conformity. On the very eve of troubles, fatal to himself and to his order, the Bishops of several extensive dioceses were able to report to him that not a single dissenter was to be found within their jurisdiction.

The tribunals afforded no protection to the subject against the civil and ecclesiastical tyranny of that period. The judges of the common law, holding their situations during the pleasure of the King, were scandalously obsequious. Yet, obsequious as they were, they were less ready and efficient instruments of arbitrary power than a class of courts, the memory of which is still, after the lapse of more than two centuries, held in deep abhorrence by the nation. Foremost among these courts in power and in infamy were the Star Chamber and the High Commission, the former a political, the latter a religious inquisition. Neither was a part of the old constitution of England. The Star Chamber had been remodelled, and the High Commission created by the Tudors. The power which these boards had possessed before the accession of Charles had been extensive and formidable, but had been small indeed when compared with that which they now usurped. Guided chiefly by the violent spirit of the primate, and freed from the control of Parliament they displayed a rapacity, a violence, a malignant energy, which had been unknown to any former age. The government was able, through their instrumentality, to fine, imprison, pillory, and mutilate without restraint. . . .

The government of England was now, in all points but one, as despotic as that of France. But that one point was all important. There was still no standing army. There was, therefore, no security that the whole fabric of tyranny might not be subverted in a single day; and, if taxes were imposed by the royal authority for the support of an army, it was probable that there would be an immediate and irresistible explosion. This was the difficulty which more than any other perplexed Wentworth. The Lord Keeper Finch, in concert with other lawyers who were employed by the government, recommended an expedient, which was eagerly adopted. The ancient princes of England, as they called on the inhabitants of the counties near Scotland to arm and array themselves for the defence of the border, had sometimes called on the maritime counties to furnish ships for the defence of the coast. In the room of [in lieu of] ships money had sometimes been accepted. This old practice it was now determined, after a long interval, not only to revive but to extend. Former princes had raised shipmoney only in time of war; it was now enacted in a time of profound peace. Former princes, even in the most perilous wars, had raised shipmoney only

along the coasts; it was now exacted from the inland shires. Former princes had raised shipmoney only for the maritime defence of the country; it was now exacted, by the admission of the Royalists themselves, with the object, not of maintaining a navy, but of furnishing the King with supplies which might be increased at his discretion to any amount, and expended at his discretion for any purpose.

The whole nation was alarmed and incensed. John Hampden, an opulent and well-born gentleman of Buckinghamshire, highly considered in his own neighbourhood, but as yet little known to the kingdom generally, had the courage to step forward, to confront the whole power of the government, and take on himself the cost and risk of disputing the prerogative to which the King laid claim. The case was argued before the judges in the Exchequer Chamber. So strong were the arguments against the pretensions of the crown that, dependent and servile as the judges were, the majority against Hampden was the smallest possible. Still there was a majority. The interpreters of the law had pronounced that one great and productive tax might be imposed by the royal authority. Wentworth justly observed that it was impossible to vindicate their judgment except by reasons directly leading to a conclusion which they had not ventured to draw. If money might legally be raised without the consent of Parliament for the support of a fleet, it was not easy to deny that money might, without consent of Parliament, be legally raised for the support of an army. . . .

And now Wentworth exulted in the near prospect of Thorough. A few years might probably suffice for the execution of his great design. If strict economy were observed, if all collision with foreign powers were carefully avoided, the debts of the crown would be cleared off: there would be funds available for the support of a large military force; and that force would soon break the refractory spirit of the nation. [Then came the uprising in Scotland, provoked by Charles I's religious policy.

The Scots invaded England, and the need for money, to raise forces to repel them, led to the summoning in 1640 first of the "Short Parliament," then of the more famous "Long Parliament."]

In November 1640 met that renowned Parliament which, in spite of many errors and disasters, is justly entitled to the reverence and gratitude of all who, in any part of the world, enjoy the blessings of constitutional government.

During the year which followed, no very important division of opinion appeared in the Houses. The civil and ecclesiastical administration had, through a period of near twelve years, been so oppressive and so unconstitutional that even those classes of which the inclinations are generally on the side of order and authority were eager to promote popular reforms, and to bring the instruments of tyranny to justice. It was enacted that no interval of more than three years should ever elapse between Parliament and Parliament, and that, if writs under the Great Seal were not issued at the proper time, the returning officers should, without such writs, call the constituent bodies together for the choice of representatives. The Star Chamber, the High Commission, the Council of York were swept away. Men who, after suffering cruel mutilations, had been confined in remote dungeons, regained their liberty. On the chief ministers of the crown the vengeance of the nation was unsparingly wreaked. The Lord Keeper, the Primate, the Lord Lieutenant were impeached. Finch saved himself by flight. Laud was flung into the Tower. Strafford was impeached, and at length put to death by act of attainder. On the same day on which this act passed, the King gave his assent to a law by which he bound himself not to adjourn, prorogue, or dissolve the existing Parliament without its own consent.

After ten months of assiduous toil, the Houses, in September 1641, adjourned for a short vacation, and the King visited Scotland. He with difficulty pacified that kingdom by consenting not only to relinquish his plans of ecclesiastical reform, but even to pass, with a very bad grace, an act declaring that episcopacy was contrary to the word of God.

When rival parties first appeared in a distinct form [after the reassembling of Parliament in October] they seemed to be not unequally matched. On the side of the government was a large majority of the nobles, and of those opulent and well descended gentlemen to whom nothing was wanting of nobility but the name. These, with the dependents whose support they could command, were no small power in the state. On the same side were the great body of the clergy, both the Universities, and all those laymen who were strongly attached to episcopal government and to the Anglican ritual. These respectable classes found themselves in the company of some allies much less decorous than themselves. The Puritan austerity drove to the King's faction all who made pleasure their business, who affected gallantry, splendour of dress, or taste in the lighter arts. With these went all who live by amusing the leisure of others, from the painter and the comic poet, down to the ropedancer and the Merry Andrew. For these artists well knew that they might thrive under a superb and luxurious despotism, but must starve under the rigid rule of the precisians. In the same interest were the Roman Catholics to a man. The Queen, a daughter of France, was of their own faith. Her husband was known to be strongly attached to her, and not a little in awe of her. Though undoubtedly a Protestant on conviction, he regarded the professors of the old religion with no ill will, and would gladly have granted them a much larger toleration than he was disposed to concede to the Presbyterians. If the opposition obtained the mastery, it was probable that the sanguinary laws enacted against Papists, in the reign of Elizabeth, would be severely enforced. The Roman Catholics were therefore induced by the strongest motives to espouse the cause of the court. They in general acted with a caution which brought on them the reproach of cowardice and lukewarmness; but it is probable that, in maintaining great reserve, they consulted the King's interest as well as their own. It was not for his service that they should be conspicuous among his friends.

The main strength of the opposition lay among the small freeholders in the country, and among the merchants and shopkeepers of the towns. But these were headed by a formidable minority of the aristocracy, a minority which included the rich and powerful Earls of Northumberland, Bedford, Warwick, Stamford, and Essex, and several other Lords of great wealth and influence. In the same ranks was found the whole body of the Protestant Nonconformists, and most of those members of the Established Church who still adhered to the Calvinistic opinions which, forty years before, had been generally held by the prelates and clergy. The municipal corporations took, with few exceptions, the same side. In the House of Commons the opposition preponderated, but not very decidedly.

Neither party wanted strong arguments for the measures which it was disposed to take. The reasonings of the most enlightened Royalists may be summed up thus: "It is true that great abuses have existed; but they have been redressed. It is true that precious rights have been invaded; but they have been vindicated and surrounded with new securities. The sittings of the Estates of the realm have been, in defiance of all precedent and of the spirit of the constitution, intermitted during eleven years; but it has now been provided that henceforth three years shall never elapse without a Parliament. The Star Chamber, the High Commission, the Council of York, oppressed and plundered us; but those hateful courts have now ceased to exist. The Lord Lieutenant aimed at establishing military despotism; but he has answered for his treason with his head. The Primate tainted our worship with Popish rites, and punished our scruples with Popish cruelty; but he is awaiting in the Tower the judgment of his peers. The Lord

Keeper sanctioned a plan, by which the property of every man in England was placed at the mercy of the crown; but he has been disgraced, ruined, and compelled to take refuge in a foreign land. The ministers of tyranny have expiated their crimes. The victims of tyranny have been compensated for their sufferings. Under such circumstances it would be most unwise to persevere in that course which was justifiable and necessary when we first met, after a long interval, and found the whole administration one mass of abuses. It is time to take heed that we do not so pursue our victory over despotism as to run into anarchy. It was not in our power to overturn the bad institutions which lately afflicted our country, without shocks which have loosened the foundations of government. Now that those institutions have fallen we must hasten to prop the edifice which it was lately our duty to batter. Henceforth it will be our wisdom to look with jealousy on schemes of innovation, and to guard from encroachment all the prerogatives with which the law has, for the public good, armed the sovereign."

Such were the views of those men of whom the excellent Falkland may be regarded as the leader. It was contended on the other side with not less force, by men of not less ability and virtue, that the safety which the liberties of the English people enjoyed was rather apparent than real, and that the arbitrary projects of the court would be resumed as soon as the vigilance of the Commons was relaxed. True it was — such was the reasoning of Pym, of Hollis, and of Hampden — that many good laws had been passed: but, if good laws had been sufficient to restrain the King, his subjects would have had little reason ever to complain of his administration. The recent statutes were surely not of more authority than the Great Charter or the Petition of Right. Yet neither the Great Charter, hallowed by the reverence of four centuries, nor the Petition of Right, sanctioned, after mature reflection, and for valuable consideration, by Charles himself, had been found effectual for the protection of the people. If once the check of fear were withdrawn, if once the spirit of opposition were suffered to slumber, all the securities for English freedom resolved themselves into a single one, the royal word; and it had been proved by a long and severe experience that the royal word could not be trusted.

The truth seems to be that [Charles] detested both the parties into which the House of Commons was divided: nor is this strange; for in both those parties the love of liberty and the love of order were mingled, though in different proportions. The advisers whom necessity had compelled him to call around him were by no means men after his own heart. They had joined in condemning his tyranny, in abridging his power, and in punishing his instruments. They were now indeed prepared to defend by strictly legal means his strictly legal prerogatives; but they would have recoiled with horror from the thought of reviving Wentworth's projects of Thorough. They were, therefore, in the King's opinion, traitors, who differed only in the degree of their seditious malignity from Pym and Hampden.

He accordingly, a few days after he had promised the chiefs of the constitutional Royalists that no step of importance should be taken without their knowledge, formed a resolution the most momentous of his whole life, carefully concealed that resolution from them, and executed it in a manner which overwhelmed them with shame and dismay. He sent the Attorney General to impeach Pym, Hollis, Hampden, and other members of the House of Commons at the bar of the House of Lords. Not content with this flagrant violation of the Great Charter and of the uninterrupted practice of centuries, he went in person, accompanied by armed men, to seize the leaders of the opposition within the walls of Parliament.

The attempt failed. The accused members had left the House a short time before Charles entered it. A sudden and violent revulsion of feeling, both in the Parliament and in the country, followed. The most favourable view that has ever been taken of the King's conduct on this occasion by his most partial advocates is that he had weakly suffered himself to be hurried into a gross indiscretion by the evil counsels of his wife and of his courtiers. But the general voice loudly charged him with far deeper guilt. At the very moment at which his subjects, after a long estrangement produced by his maladministration, were returning to him with feelings of confidence and affection, he had aimed a deadly blow at all their dearest rights, at the privileges of Parliament, at the very principle of trial by jury. He had shown that he considered opposition to his arbitrary designs as a crime to be expiated only by blood. He had broken faith, not only with his Great Council and with his people, but with his own adherents. He had done what, but for an unforeseen accident, would probably have produced a bloody conflict round the Speaker's chair. Those who had the chief sway in the Lower House now felt that not only their power and popularity, but their lands and their necks, were staked on the event of the struggle in which they were engaged. . . .

He quitted London, never to return till the day of a terrible and memorable reckoning had arrived. A negotiation began which occupied many months. Accusations and recriminations passed backward and forward between the contending parties. All accommodation had become impossible. The sure punishment which waits on habitual perfidy had at length overtaken the King. It was to no purpose that he now pawned his royal word, and invoked heaven to witness the sincerity of his professions. The distrust with which his adversaries regarded him was not to be removed by oaths or treaties. They were convinced that they could be safe only when he was utterly helpless. Their demand, therefore, was, that he should surrender, not only those prerogatives which he had usurped in violation of ancient laws and of his own recent promises, but also other prerogatives which the English Kings had possessed from time immemorial, and continue to possess at the present day. No minister must be appointed, no peer created without the consent of the Houses. Above all, the sovereign must resign that supreme military authority which, from time beyond all memory, had appertained to the regal office. . . .

When a country is in the situation in which England then was, when the kingly office is regarded with love and veneration, but the person who fills that office is hated and distrusted, it should seem that the course which ought to be taken is obvious. The dignity of the office should be preserved; the person should be discarded. Thus our ancestors acted in 1399 and in 1689. Had there been, in 1642, any man occupying a position similar to that which Henry of Lancaster occupied at the time of the deposition of Richard the Second,

and which the Prince of Orange occupied at the time of the deposition of James the Second, it is probable that the Houses would have changed the dynasty, and would have made no formal change in the constitution. The new King, called to the throne by their choice, and dependent on their support, would have been under the necessity of governing in conformity with their wishes and opinions. But there was no prince of the blood royal in the parliamentary party; and, though that party contained many men of high rank and many men of eminent ability, there was none who towered so conspicuously above the rest that he could be proposed as a candidate for the crown. As there was to be a King, and as no new King was to be found, it was necessary to leave the regal title to Charles. Only one course, therefore, was left: and that was to disjoin the regal title from the regal prerogatives.

The English Bourgeois Revolution:
A Marxist Interpretation

CHRISTOPHER HILL

Apart from war service, and a year in the Soviet Union, Christopher Hill (born 1912) has spent most of his working life at Oxford, where he is now Fellow of Balliol College. His most important work has been on the economic problems of the Church of England in the half century before the Civil War, but he has also written many essays on the period. *The English Revolution,* from which this excerpt is taken, was published as a Marxist textbook.

Tʜᴇ most usual explanation of the seventeenth-century revolution is one that was put forward by the leaders of the Parliament of 1640 themselves in their propaganda statements and appeals to the people. It has been repeated with additional

detail and adornments by Whig and Liberal historians ever since. This explanation says that the Parliamentary armies were fighting for the liberty of the individual and his rights in law against a tyrannical government that threw him into prison

From Christopher Hill, *The English Revolution* (London, 1955), pp. 7–9, 10–11, 11–12, 26–27, 28–33, 39–44. By permission of Lawrence & Wishart, Ltd.

without trial by jury, taxed him without asking his consent, billeted soldiers in his house, robbed him of his property, and attempted to destroy his cherished Parliamentary institutions. Now all this is true — as far as it goes. The Stuarts did try to stop people meeting and holding political discussions, did cut off the ears of people who criticised the government, did arbitrarily collect taxes which were very unequal in their incidence, did try to shut up Parliament and rule the country by nominated officials. All this is true. And although Parliament in the seventeenth century was even less genuinely representative of ordinary people than it is at the present day, still its victory was important as establishing a certain amount of self-government for the richer classes in society.

But further questions are still unanswered. Why did the King become tyrannical? Why did the landed and commercial classes represented in Parliament have to fight for their liberties? During the sixteenth century, under the Tudor rulers, the grandfathers of the Parliamentarians of 1640 were the monarchy's stoutest supporters. What had happened to change their outlook? Parliament had supported Henry VII and Henry VIII and Elizabeth in their efforts to police the country against the anarchy and brigandage of overmighty subjects, of feudal potentates with their private armies, and England had been made safe for commercialism. Parliament had also supported Henry VIII and Elizabeth in their victorious struggle against the international Catholic Church: money no longer went from England to Rome, British policy was no longer dictated by the interests of a foreign power. Parliament, finally, encouraged Queen Elizabeth in her resistance to the political ally of the Papacy, the Spanish Empire; and the plunder of the New World was thrown open to Drake, Hawkins, and the piratical but Protestant seadogs.

The Tudors, in short, were backed by the politically effective classes because the latter did very well out of Tudor rule. Why did the Stuarts, James I and Charles I, lose this support? It was not just because James, who succeeded Elizabeth in 1603, was a particularly stupid man, a Scot who did not understand England, though many historians have seriously argued thus. But one has only to read what James, Charles and their supporters wrote and said, or examine what they did, to see that so far from being merely stupid, they were either able men trying to impose a vicious policy, or men whose ideas were hopelessly out of date and therefore reactionary. The causes of the civil war must be sought in society, not in individuals.

Another school of historians — which we may call "Tory" as opposed to the Whigs — holds that the royal policy was not tyrannical at all, that Charles I, as he told the court which sentenced him to death, spoke "not of my own right alone, as I am your King, but for the true liberty of all my subjects." Clarendon, who deserted the Parliament in 1642 and later became Charles II's first minister, developed this theory in several volumes of eloquent prose in his *History of the Great Rebellion;* it is now propagated by a number of historians whose political prejudices, royalist or Catholic sympathies, and bias against liberalism in general, make up for their lack of historical understanding. Their idea is that Charles I and his advisers were really trying to protect ordinary people from economic exploitation by a small class of capitalists on the make; and that the opposition to Charles was organised and worked up to serve their own purposes by those business men who identified their interests with the House of Commons in politics and Puritanism in religion.

Now, it is true that the English Revolution of 1640, like the French Revolution of 1789, was a struggle for political, economic, and religious power, waged by the middle class, the bourgeoisie, which grew in wealth and strength as capitalism developed. But it is not true that as against them the royal government stood for the interests of the common people: on the contrary, the popular parties proved to be the King's most militant opponents, far more vigorous and ruthless and thorough-going than the bourgeoisie itself.

The interests for which Charles's monarchy stood were not those of the common people at all. It represented the landowning nobles, and its policy was influenced by a Court clique of aristocratic commercial racketeers and their hangers-on, sucking the life-blood from the whole people by methods of economic exploitation which we shall be considering later on. The middle-class struggle to shake off the control of this group was not merely selfish; it fulfilled a progressive historical function. The sharper-witted landowners were grafting themselves as parasites on to the new growth of capitalism, since their own mode of economic existence no longer sufficed to maintain them. It was necessary for the further development of capitalism that this choking parasitism should be ended by the overthrow of the feudal state. It was to the advantage of the masses of the population that capitalism should be allowed to develop freely. Under the old order, in the century before 1640, real wages for labourers in industry and agriculture fell by more than one half: in the century after 1640 they more than doubled.

A third theory is emphasised by both sides: that the conflict was to decide which of two religions, Puritanism or Anglicanism, was to be dominant in England. Here, again, the effect of this explanation is to make us pity and misunderstand the men of the seventeenth century, and congratulate ourselves on being so much more sensible to-day: however much Anglicans and Nonconformists may dislike one another personally, we say, they no longer fight in the village street. But this is to miss the point. Certainly religious squabbles fill many pages of the pamphlet literature of the seventeenth century: both sides justified their attitude ultimately in religious terms, believing they were fighting God's battles. But "religion" covered something much wider than it does to-day. The

Church throughout the Middle Ages, and down to the seventeenth century, was something very different from what we call a Church to-day. It guided all the movements of men from baptism to the burial service, and was the gateway to that life to come in which all men fervently believed. The Church educated children; in the village parishes — where the mass of the people were illiterate — the parson's sermon was the main source of information on current events and problems, of guidance on economic conduct. The parish itself was an important unit of local government, collecting and doling out such pittances as the poor received. The Church controlled men's feelings and told them what to believe, provided them with entertainment and shows. It took the place of news and propaganda services now covered by many different and more efficient institutions — the Press, the B.B.C., the cinema, the club, and so forth; it is also why the government often told preachers exactly what to preach.

The Church, then, defended the existing order, and it was important for the Government to maintain its control over this publicity and propaganda agency. For the same reason, those who wanted to overthrow the feudal state had to attack and seize control of the Church. That is why political theories tended to get wrapped up in religious language. It was not that our seventeenth-century forefathers were much more conscientious and saintly men than we are. Whatever may be true of Ireland or Spain, we in England to-day can see our problems in secular terms just because our ancestors put an end to the use of the Church as an exclusive and persecuting instrument of political power. We can be sceptical and tolerant in religious matters, not because we are wiser and better, but because Cromwell, stabling in cathedrals the horses of the most disciplined and most democratic cavalry the world had yet seen, won a victory which for ever stopped men being flogged and branded for having unorthodox views about the Communion service. As long as the power of the State was weak and uncentralised the Church with its parson in every parish, the parson with honoured access to every household, could tell people what to believe and how to behave; and behind the threats and censures of the Church were all the terrors of hell fire. Under these circumstances social conflicts inevitably became religious conflicts.

But the fact that men spoke and wrote in religious language should not prevent us from realising that there is a social content behind what are apparently purely theological ideas. Each class created and sought to impose the religious outlook best suited to its own needs and interests. But the real clash is between these class interests: behind the parson stood the squire.

It is not then denied that the "Puritan Revolution" was a religious as well as a political struggle; but it was more than that. What men were fighting about was the whole nature and future development of English society.

The point to be stressed is this. There was a great deal of capital in England which merchants, yeomen and gentlemen were anxious to invest in the freest possible industrial, commercial, and agricultural development. This was continually thwarted by feudal survivals in town and country, and by government policy deliberately endeavouring in the interests of the old landed ruling class to restrict production and the accumulation of capital. Thus, in attacking the feudal landlords' state and the oligarchy of big merchants in alliance with the Court who were trying to monopolise business profits, the struggle of the bourgeoisie was progressive, representing the interests of the country as a whole.

England in 1640 was still ruled by landlords and the relations of production were still partly feudal, but there was this vast and expanding capitalist sector, whose development the Crown and feudal landlords could not for ever hold in check. There were few proletarians (except in London), most of the producers under the putting-out system being also small peasants. But these peasants and small artisans were losing their independence. They were hit especially hard by the general rise in prices, and were being brought into ever closer dependence on the merchants and squires. A statute of 1563 forbad the poorer 75 per cent of the rural population to go as apprentices into industry.

So there were really three classes in conflict. As against the parasitic feudal landowners and speculative financiers, as against the government whose policy was to restrict and control industrial expansion, the interests of the new class of capitalist merchants and farmers were temporarily identical with those of the small peasantry and artisans and journeymen. But conflict between the two latter classes was bound to develop, since this expansion of capitalism involved the dissolution of the old agrarian and industrial relationships and the transformation of independent small masters and peasants into proletarians.

Until about 1590, the monarchy had many interests in common with those of the bourgeoisie in town and country — in the struggle against Spain, against the international Catholic Church, against rival noble houses disputing supreme control with the House of Tudor and ruining the country with their private wars. Hence the collaboration in Parliament between monarchy, gentry, and bourgeoisie. Yet ultimately the unity of interest broke down.

Up to a point, indeed, the bourgeoisie and the feudal gentry were able to get along together under the monarchy. In an age when plunder and piracy helped in the rapid accumulation of capital, the reckless seadogs of the semi-feudal south-western counties — Devon and Cornwall — heaped up wealth on a scale which the more cautious merchants of London could never have imitated. In looting Spanish colonies and Spanish treasure ships for gold, in the quest for land in Ireland and North America, the adventurers of the decaying class did not come into conflict with the rising entrepreneurs. Those who were fortunate acquired the capital necessary to take part in production for the market themselves: the lines of class division had not yet crystallised.

This hardening process took place in the reigns of James I and Charles I. By then the new landed gentry and respectable traders wished to settle down to peaceful development and legitimate trade. "The new age had turned its back on the gold which did not come through chartered companies." "Peace and law have beggared us all," wailed the future royalist Sir John Oglander.

So the feudal gentry, as their incomes from land declined, became more and more dependent on the Court for jobs and economic pickings, more and more parasitic. As the Stuart monarchy became progressively less useful to the bourgeoisie, so it became more indispensable to the aristocracy and courtiers, their only guarantee of economic survival. That is why they were to fight for it so desperately in the Civil War.

For the monarchy was bound up with the feudal order by more than the bonds of conservative sentiment. The King himself was the greatest of feudal landlords and, though he was in a better position than others to get a rake-off from the new capitalist wealth, he was opposed no less than any other landowner to a fundamental change from a feudal to a capitalist order of society.

In the early sixteenth century the monarchy had used the bourgeoisie as an ally against its most powerful rivals — the other great feudal houses weakened by the Wars of the Roses and the Church. The alliance between Crown and Parliament (representing the landed classes and the merchants) had in the early sixteenth century been genuine. The new men prospered under the shelter of the throne; the monarchy defended them from internal reaction or revolt, as when it defeated the Pilgrimage of Grace (1536) and the rising of the northern earls (1569). The Crown also defended them from the external reactionary power of Spain (the Armada). The only time when reaction seemed for a brief

period likely to triumph was when Queen Mary was married to Philip of Spain; and then the terror and burnings with which alone her policy could be carried through helped to confirm the national hatred of Catholicism. So the collaboration between Crown and Parliament in the Tudor period was based on a community of real interests. The Parliamentary franchise was very restricted and the House of Commons represented exclusively the landed class and the merchants, while the House of Lords remained the more important chamber until the Commons seized the initiative in James I's reign. Parliament under the Tudors did not meet often, and then normally approved royal policy.

But by the last decade of the sixteenth century, when all its internal and external foes had been crushed, the bourgeoisie ceased to depend on the protection of the monarchy; at the same time the Crown became increasingly aware of the dangerous possibilities of the growing wealth of the bourgeoisie, and strove to consolidate its position before it was too late.

This clash can be seen in the quarrels of James I and Charles I with their Parliaments. The change was in the relative strength of the class forces; James was sillier than Elizabeth, but this alone does not account for the failure of his policy where hers succeeded. James formulated grandiose theories of the divine right of kings where Elizabeth had preserved a prudent silence; but this is a symptom of the growing divergence between Crown and Parliament, not a cause. James had to define his position because it was being called in question. The real crux of the problem was finance, over which there had already been conflict at the end of Elizabeth's reign. Prices were rising, the wealth of the bourgeoisie was increasing by leaps and bounds, yet the revenue of the Crown, as of most great landowners, remained static and inadequate to the new needs. Unless the Crown could tap the new wealth either (a) by drastically increasing taxation at the expense of the bourgeoisie and gentry, or (b) by somehow taking part in the productive process itself, its independent power must disappear.

The first policy — increased customs, forced loans, new taxes — led to violent quarrels with Parliament, which had long claimed the right to control taxation, and was not going to allow taxes to be increased unless it was given full control over the machinery of state.

The second policy led to the erection of monopolies in the attempt to control certain industries and obtain a rentier's rake-off from that control, e.g. coal, alum, soap, etc. It outraged the whole business population, capitalists and employees alike. The scandal reached its height in "Cockayne's project" (1616). This was a scheme to bring the clothing industry under royal control and expand exports to the advantage of the Exchequer. It was sabotaged by the exporters, and led to a crisis of over-production and widespread unemployment, the blame for which attached itself to the Crown.

A third policy, tried by the Stuarts after all others had failed, never had a chance of success. This was an attempt to revive and increase the revenue from feudal dues. There was no chance of the Crown becoming financially independent of the bourgeoisie from this source alone; the only consequence of its exploitation was the alienation of the Crown's potential friends among the aristocracy and gentry, as well as of the bourgeoisie. For with the increasing economic difficulties, and the political threat from the bourgeoisie, the monarchy was thrown back on the exclusive support of the nobility and the economically unprogressive, parasitic elements in the state. On the other side, the nobility itself came to depend more and more on the Crown's control of economic life to maintain its own position. It wanted Court patronage for its landless younger sons, whom bourgeois competition was driving out of the professions; it wanted privileges and monopolies which would give it a rentier's share in the profits of developing capitalism. It is not surprising that the major parliamentary clashes of the early seventeenth century were over this very issue of monopolies. They were the means by which the monarchy attempted to control and canalise commercial activity in the interests of the greedy courtiers, the "drones," in denunciation of whom Puritan sermons abounded.

Another great landowner remains to be considered, whose interests were even more closely bound up with those of the monarchy — the Church hierarchy. Since the dissolution of the monasteries, the remaining possessions of the Church of England were coveted by a section of the gentry. Only the usefulness of the bishops to the Crown protected the Church from further spoliation. Its moral authority, too, could now no longer be drawn from the international Papacy with which Henry VIII had broken, but only from the national monarchy, its only defender against Catholic reaction and left-wing Protestant revolutionaries. So the Elizabethan Church stood for passive obedience to divinely constituted authority, and preached that rebellion was the worst possible sin. The dependence of the Church on the Crown was a century old by 1640, and their alliance was based on the closest community of interest. As the breach between Crown and bourgeoisie widened, so the Puritan attack on the Church, on its forms and ceremonies, its courts and discipline, became hardly distinguishable from the Parliamentary attack on the Crown. A group of merchants in London formed a society for establishing lectureships in the "barren parts" of the country, and lecturers nominated by town corporations incurred the special hostility of Charles I's Archbishop, Laud, who rightly suspected that their theology and political theory would be equally "unsound" from the point of view of the Government.

Two social systems and their ideologies were in conflict. Presbyterianism (which advocated abolition of the royally appointed bishops and the domination of each Church by elders — local bigwigs) was an oligarchical theory which especially appealed to the big bourgeoisie. What they wanted was a

Church organised in such a way as to be capable of diffusing throughout the whole of society the political and economic ways of thinking convenient for the merchant class. For it has been abundantly demonstrated how the morality that Puritanism preached was precisely the outlook needed for the accumulation of capital and the expansion of capitalism. The emphasis was on thrift, sobriety, hard work in the station to which God hath called a man; an unceasing labour in whatever calling, merchant or artisan, one happened to be, but with no extravagant enjoyment of the fruits of labour, and unceasing preoccupation with duty to the detriment of "worldly" pleasure. The wealthy were to accumulate capital, the poor to labour at their tasks — as a divine duty and always under the "great Task-master's" eye. This belief inspired the bourgeoisie to remodel society in the divinely ordained fashion as God's "elect," and if that fashion bore a striking resemblance to the capitalist system, they were ever more firmly convinced that they were doing the work of God and that ultimate victory was both predestined and assured. Their conviction of "salvation" was born of the historical necessity and progressiveness of their task, and was confirmed by the material prosperity with which God tended to bless his servants.

The hierarchy counter-attacked by trying to increase tithe payments in the towns, and to recover some of the Church's lost revenues (tithes which had been "impropriated" — that is to say, diverted into the pockets of a lay landlord from the ecclesiastical purposes for which they had formerly been charged on all occupiers of property). At the same time, it tried to extend its control over patronage in order to appoint to Church livings socially and doctrinally acceptable incumbents. "Subversive" views on doctrine and discipline were ruthlessly punished by the ecclesiastical Court of High Commission, with Laud at its head. The Puritan opposition depicted the whole trend of Charles's policy as a return to papistry, which is truer in spirit than in the letter. Laud was no doctrinal papist,

and he refused all overtures from Rome; but the social policy which he personified was an attempt to revive and perpetuate obsolete medieval economic and social relationships and the ways of thinking corresponding to them. Thus the fight to control the Church was of fundamental importance; whoever controlled its doctrine and organisation was in a position to determine the nature of society. James I was making a shrewd political analysis when he said, "No Bishop, No King." It was only three years after the abolition of episcopacy that Charles I died on the scaffold.

This [the Long] Parliament differed from its predecessors only in the length of its session. It represented the same classes — principally the gentry and wealthy merchants. Consequently it came to reflect the division among the English gentry corresponding roughly to the economic division between feudal north-west and capitalist south-east. But the House of Commons did not make the Revolution: its members were subject to pressure from outside, from the people of London, the yeomen and artisans of the home counties.

But in 1640 most classes were united against the Crown. The final issues were: (a) destruction of the bureaucratic machinery whereby the Government had been able to rule in contravention of the desires of the great majority of its politically influential subjects (Strafford was executed, Laud imprisoned, other leading Ministers fled abroad; the Star Chamber, Court of High Commission, and other prerogative courts were abolished); (b) prevention of a standing army controlled by the King; (c) abolition of the recent financial expedients, whose aim had also been to render the King independent of the control of the bourgeoisie in Parliament, and whose effect had been economic dislocation and the undermining of confidence; (d) Parliamentary (i.e. bourgeois) control of the Church, so that it could no longer be used as a reactionary propaganda agency.

A crisis was forced by a revolt in Ireland in 1641. With the withdrawal of Strafford, the English Government there, which had long been oppressive, ceased to be strong, and the Irish seized the opportunity to attempt to throw off the English yoke. Parliament was united in its determination to keep the first British colony in subjection; but the bourgeoisie firmly refused to trust Charles with an army for its re-conquest (Royalist plots in the armed forces had already been exposed). So Parliament was reluctantly forced to take control of the Army.

The unanimity inside Parliament came to an end. To most of the aristocracy and conservative gentry, the policy of the leaders of the House of Commons, and especially their readiness to appeal to public opinion outside Parliament, seemed leading to a break-up of the social order in which their dominant position was secure, and they gradually fell back to support the King. In the country as a whole, division went along broad class lines. The landed class was divided, many being frightened by riots against enclosures and threats of a peasant revolt, such as had shaken the Midlands in 1607; the progressive section of the gentry and the bourgeoisie were confident that they could ride the storm. In London, whilst monopolists and the ruling oligarchy supported the Court from which their profits came, the main body of merchants, artisans, and apprentices gave active support to the forward party in Parliament, and pushed it steadily further along the revolutionary path. The great leader of the Commons, Pym, welcomed this popular support, and in the Grand Remonstrance (November, 1641) the revolutionary leaders drew up a sweeping indictment of Charles's Government, and published it for propaganda purposes — a new technique of appeal to the people.

But the decision to print the Remonstrance had been the occasion of a savage clash in the House and was passed by only eleven votes, after which the division became irreconcilable. The future Royalists withdrew from Parliament, not (as is often alleged) because of their devotion to bishops, but rather (as a Member said in the debate) because, "if we make a parity in the Church we must come to a parity in the Commonwealth." If the property of the ecclesiastical landlords could be confiscated, whose turn might not come next? The big bourgeoisie itself was frightened, and felt the need of some kind of monarchical settlement (with a reformed monarchy responsive to its interests) to check the flow of popular feeling. It tried desperately to stem the revolutionary torrent it had let loose. One gentleman switched over from the side of Parliament to the King because he feared that "the necessitous people of the whole kingdom will presently rise in mighty numbers; and whosoever they pretend for at first, within a while they will set up for themselves, to the utter ruin of all the nobility and gentry of the kingdom." "Rich men," a pamphleteer ironically observed later, "are none of the greatest enemies to monarchy." But this fear of the common people only encouraged the King to think himself indispensable: he refused all overtures, and in the summer of 1642 war began.

In time of war men must choose one side or the other. Many gentlemen to whom property meant more than principle chose the line of least resistance and saved their estates by cooperating with whichever party dominated in their area. But even among the men of conviction, the dividing issues were obscured (as they have been for many historians) by the fact that many of the hated State officials were also officials of the national Church. And for the Church much traditional and sentimental popularity could be worked up. Many of the Parliamentarians, moreover, tended to speak as though they thought the most important part of their struggle the ideological battle of Puritanism against an Anglicanism that was barely distinguishable from Catholicism. But their actions make it clear that they knew that more than this was at stake.

The issue was one of political power. The bourgeoisie had rejected Charles I's Government, not because he was a bad man, but because he represented an obsolete social system. His Government tried to perpetuate a feudal social order when the conditions existed for freer capitalist development, when the increase in national wealth could come only by means of free capitalist development. A seventeenth-century parson thus described the line-up: "Against the king, the laws and religion, were a company of poor tradesmen, broken and decayed citizens, deluded and priest-ridden women, . . . the rude rabble that knew not wherefore they were got together . . . tailors, shoemakers, link-boys, etc.; . . . on the king's side, . . . all the bishops of the land, all the deans, prebends, and learned men; both the universities; all the princes, dukes, marquises; all the earls and lords except two or three; all the knights and gentlemen in the three nations, except a score of sectaries and atheists." We need not take that partisan account too literally, but it makes the *class* nature of the division clear.

Charles's policy throughout his reign illustrates the class basis of his rule. He tried to regulate trade and industry with the contradictory intention both of slowing down a too rapid capitalist development and of sharing in its profits. In foreign policy he wished for the alliance of the most reactionary powers, Spain and Austria, and refused therefore the forward national policy demanded by the bourgeoisie. Because he lost all favour with the moneyed classes, he had to levy illegal taxes, to aim to dispense with Parliament, to rule by force. His failure in Scotland showed up the rottenness of the whole structure which he had reared; and his appeals for national unity against the foreign enemy fell on deaf ears. The real enemy was at home. The invading Scottish army was hailed as an ally. The Parliamentarian attack showed that the opposition had realised that they were fighting more than a few evil counsellors (as they had long believed or pretended to believe), more even than the King himself. They

were fighting a system. Before the social order they needed could be secure they had to smash the old bureaucratic machinery, defeat the cavaliers in battle. The heads of a king and many peers had to roll in the dust before it could be certain that future kings and the peerage would recognise the dominance of the new class.

For many years during and after the Civil War, in their eagerness to defeat the old order, the moneyed classes willingly accepted taxes three or four times as heavy as those they had refused to pay to Charles I. For the objection was not to taxes as such; it was to the policy to implement which taxes were collected. The bourgeoisie had no confidence in Charles, would not trust him with money, because they knew that the whole basis of his rule was hostile to their development. But to a government of their own kind the purse-strings were at once loosed.

Nor was it a war of the rich only. All sections of society in southern and eastern England brought in their contributions to help win the war, for in the overthrow of the old regime men saw the essential preliminary condition of social and intellectual advance. Many of those who fought for Parliament were afterwards disappointed with the achievements of the revolution, felt they had been betrayed. But they were right to fight. A victory for Charles I and his gang could only have meant the economic stagnation of England, the stabilisation of a backward feudal society in a commercial age, and have necessitated an even bloodier struggle for liberation later. The Parliamentarians thought they were fighting God's battles. They were certainly fighting those of posterity, throwing off an intolerable incubus to further advance. The fact that the revolution might have gone further should never allow us to forget the heroism and faith and disciplined energy with which ordinary decent people responded when the Parliament's leaders freely and frankly appealed to them to support its cause.

PART II: THE ORIGINS OF THE CIVIL WAR AS SEEN BY SOME CONTEMPORARIES

A Constitutional Royalist Views the Work of Extremists in the House of Commons

EDWARD HYDE, EARL OF CLARENDON

A lawyer and member of the Long Parliament, Hyde (1609–74) at first voted with the reforming majority, and even helped to prepare the articles for Strafford's impeachment. Rallying to the defense of King and Church late in 1641, he became one of Charles I's principal advisers at Oxford during the Civil War. In exile from 1646 to 1660 in Jersey and France, he returned to England as Charles II's Lord Chancellor. Falling from power in 1667, he went again into exile in France, and died at Rouen. The *History* was written in the last years of his life, but was in part based upon a version compiled at the beginning of his first exile.

W HEN this work [Strafford's imprisonment after he had been impeached] was so prosperously over, they [the extremists in Parliament] began to consider, that notwithstanding all the industry that had been used to procure such members to be chosen, or returned though not chosen, who had been most refractory to the government of the church and state; yet that the house was so constituted, that when the first heat (which almost all men brought with them) should be a little allayed, violent counsels would not be long hearkened to: and therefore, as they took great care by their committee of elections to remove as many of those members as they suspected not to be inclinable to their passions upon pretense "that they were not regularly chosen," that so they might bring in others more compliable in their places;

in which no rules of justice was so much as pretended to be observed by them . . . so they declared, "That no person, how lawfully and regularly soever chosen and returned, should be and sit as a member with them, who had been a party or a favourer of any project, or who had been employed in any illegal commission."

The next art was to make the severity and rigour of the house as formidable as was possible, and to make as many men apprehend themselves obnoxious to the house, as had been in any trust or employment in the kingdom. Thus they passed many general votes concerning ship-money, in which all who had been high sheriffs, and so collected it, were highly concerned. The like sharp conclusions [were made] upon all lords lieutenants and their deputies, which were the prime gentlemen of

From Edward Hyde, Earl of Clarendon, *History of the Great Rebellion* (Oxford, 1839), pp. 75, 78–9, 112–13. By permission of The Clarendon Press.

quality in all the counties of England.[1] Then upon some disquisition of the proceedings in the star-chamber, and at the council-table, all who concurred in such a sentence, and consented to such an order, were declared criminous, and to be proceeded against. So that, in a moment, all the lords of the council, all who had been deputy lieutenants, or high sheriffs, during the late years, found themselves within the mercy of these grand inquisitors: and hearing new terms of art, that a complication of several misdemeanours might grow up to treason, and the like, it was no wonder if men desired by all means to get their favour and protection.

When they had sufficiently startled men by these proceedings, and upon half an hour's debate sent up an accusation against the lord archbishop of Canterbury of high treason, and so removed him likewise from the king's council, they rested satisfied with their general rules, votes, and orders, without making haste to proceed either against things or persons; being willing rather to keep men in suspense, and to have the advantage of their fears, than, by letting them see the worst that could befall them, lose the benefit of their application. For this reason they used their utmost skill to keep off any debate of ship-money, that that whole business might hang like a meteor over the heads of those that were in any degree faulty in it. . . .

In the house of commons were many persons of wisdom and gravity, who being possessed of great and plentiful fortunes, though they were undevoted enough to the court, had all imaginable duty for the king, and affection to the government established by law or ancient custom; and without doubt, the major part of that body consisted of men who had no mind to break the peace of the kingdom, or to make any considerable alteration in the government of church or state: and therefore all inventions were

set on foot from the beginning to work on them, and corrupt them, by suggestions "of the dangers which threatened all that was precious to the subject in their liberty and property, by overthrowing or overmastering the law, and subjecting it to an arbitrary power, and by countenancing popery to the subversion of the protestant religion"; and then, by infusing terrible apprehensions into some, and so working upon their fears "of being called in question for somewhat they had done," by which they would stand in need of their protection; and raising the hopes of others, "that, by concurring with them, they should be sure to obtain offices, and honours, and any kind of preferment." Though there were too many corrupted and misled by these several temptations, and others who needed no other temptations than from the fierceness and barbarity of their own natures, and the malice they had contracted against the church and against the court; yet the number was not great of those in whom the government of the rest was vested, nor were there many who had the absolute authority to lead, though there were a multitude that was disposed to follow.

All men discerned this gross usage [the granting of tonnage and poundage, the customs duties which up to the reign of Charles I had traditionally been granted to rulers for life, for two months only, after Strafford's execution], and the disadvantage imposed upon his majesty by this mutation; and therefore expected a full reparation, by such an act for life as had been usual; and such an improvement of the book of rates as had been promised, as soon as the business of the earl of Strafford was over: which had always been objected, as necessary to precede all other consultations. But this was no sooner moved, "as seasonable in order to their own professions, and in a degree due to the king, after so many reiterated expressions of favour and affection to his people, by so many excellent laws, and other condescensions," than they objected, "the odiousness of the late plot against the parliament, which was not yet

[1] As royal officials these men had been obliged to enforce Charles' famous ship-money tax imposed without consent of Parliament in 1632. [Editor's note]

fully discovered: that notwithstanding those gracious demonstrations of favour from the king, in the laws and other acts mentioned, they had great cause to apprehend, some ill affected persons had still an influence upon his majesty, to the disservice of the parliament, and to beget jealousies in him towards them; for that they had plainly discovered (which they should in a short time be able to present fully to the house) that there had been a design, not only to poison the affections of the army towards the parliament, by making them believe that they were neglected, and the Scots preferred much before them; but to bring up that army to London, with a purpose to awe the parliament: that there was a resolution to seize the Tower, and to make it a curb upon the city: that there had been an attempt to prevail with the officers of the Scottish army, at least to sit still as neuters, whilst the other acted this tragedy: that the confederates in this design had taken an oath, to oppose any course that should be advised for the removing the bishops out of the house of peers; to preserve and defend the king's prerogative, to the utmost extent that any of his progenitors had enjoyed; and to settle his majesty's revenue: that they had reason to fear his majesty's own concurrence, at least his approbation, in this design, (which, if not prevented, must have proved so pernicious and fatal to the kingdom), for that, besides that the persons principally engaged in it were of the nearest trust about the king and queen, they had clear proof, that a paper had passed his majesty's perusal, in which were contained many sharp invectives against the parliament; a desire that they might have the exercise of martial law, (the mention whereof was the most unpopular and odious thing that could be imagined), and an offer of service to defend his majesty's person, which was an implication as if it had been in danger: and that this paper should have been signed by all the officers of the army; for their better encouragement wherein, the king himself had written a C. and an R. as a testimony that he approved of it."

This discourse, so methodically and confidently averred, made a strange impression (without reserving themselves until the evidence should be produced) in the minds of most men; who believed, that such particulars could never have been with that solemnity informed, if the proofs were not very clear; and served, not only to blast whatsoever was moved on his majesty's behalf, but to discountenance what, till then, had been the most popular motion that could be made, which was, the disbanding both armies, and the Scots' return into their own country. For the better accomplishment whereof, and as a testimony of their brotherly affection, the two houses had frankly and bountifully undertaken "to give them a gratuity of three hundred thousand pounds, over and above the twenty-five thousand pounds the month, during the time that their stay here should be necessary."

After that act, the king might have been reasonably awaked from any extraordinary confidence in the loyalty, honour, or justice, of both houses. And without doubt, when posterity shall recover the courage, and conscience, and the old honour of the English nation, it will not without more indignation and blushes contemplate any action of this seditious and rebellious age, than that the nobility and gentry of England, who were not guilty of the treason, should recompense an invasion from a foreign contemned nation, with whatever establishments they proposed in their own kingdom, and with a donative of three hundred thousand pounds, over and above all charges, out of the bowels of England; which will yet appear the more prodigious, when it shall be considered, that a fifth part of those who were accessaries to that infamous prodigality were neither favourers of their ends, or well-wishers of their nation.

After they had played with this plot, and given the house heats and colds, by applying parts of it to them upon emergent occasions, for the space of near three months; and finding, that though it did them many notable services, in advancing their own reputations, and calumniating the king's honour, yet, that it had not a through effect at court for their preferment; they resolved to shew all their ware, and to produce the whole evidence: for the perfecting whereof, they had "a late great mark of God's great favour towards them, in his furnishing them with evidence [the "edited" diary of Strafford] for the complete discovery of all the mischief, from one that was a principal contriver of it."

Puritanism and Liberty Versus Prelacy and Despotism

LUCY HUTCHINSON

> Born in 1620, she married John Hutchinson at the age of 18. He became a prominent Parliamentarian in Nottinghamshire, took part in the "trial" of Charles I, and, imprisoned for this after the Restoration, died in captivity in 1664. In the years that followed, his widow prepared his biography, not for publication but for the edification of their children. The *Life of Colonel Hutchinson* was not printed until 1806, 131 years after the probable date of Lucy's death.

WHEN the dawn of the gospel began to break upon this isle, after the dark midnight of papacy, the morning was more cloudy here than in other places by reason of the state-interest, which was mixing and working itself into the interest of religion, and which in the end quite wrought it out. King Henry the Eighth, who by his royal authority cast out the pope, did not intend the people of the land should have any ease of oppression; but only changed their foreign yoke for home-bred fetters, dividing the pope's spoils between himself and his bishops, who cared not for their father at Rome, so long as they enjoyed their patrimony and their honours here under another head: so that I cannot subscribe to those who entitle that king to the honour of the reformation. But even then there wanted not many who discerned the corruptions that were retained in the Church, and eagerly applied their endeavours to obtain a purer reformation; against whom, those who saw no need of further reformation, either through excess of joy for that which was already brought forth, or else through a secret love of superstition rooted in their hearts, thought this too much — were bitterly incensed, and, hating that light which reproved their darkness, everywhere stirred up spirits of envy and persecution against them. Upon the great revolution which took place at the accession of Queen Elizabeth to the crown, the nation became divided into three great factions, the Papists, the State-protestants, and the more religious zealots, who afterwards were branded with the name of Puritan. In vain it was for them to address the queen and the parliament; for the bishops, under the specious pretences of uniformity and obedience, procured severe

From *Memoirs of the Life of Colonel Hutchinson, Governor of Nottingham, by his widow Lucy,* ed. Charles H. Firth, 2 vols. (London, 1885), Vol. I, pp. 99–100, 117–21, 122–3, 123–4, 125–6, 126–7.

punishments to be inflicted on such as durst gainsay their determinations in all things concerning worship, whereupon some even in those godly days lost their lives.

While these parties were thus counterworking, the treasure of the kingdom [under James I] being wasted by court-caterpillars, and parliaments called to re-supply the royal coffers, therein there wanted not some, that retained so much of the English spirit as to represent the public grievances, and desire to call the corrupt ministers of state to account. But the king, grudging that his people should dare to gainsay his pleasure, and correct his misgovernment in his favourites, broke up parliaments, violated their privileges, imprisoned their members for things spoken in the house, and grew disaffected to them, and entertained projects of supply by other grievances of the people. The prelates, in the meantime, finding they lost ground, meditated reunion with the popish faction, who began to be at a pretty agreement with them; and now there was no more endeavour in their public sermons to confute the errors of that church, but to reduce our doctrines and theirs to an accommodation. The king, to bring it about, was deluded into the treaty of a match for his son with the Infanta of Spain; and the prince, with the Duke of Buckingham, was privately sent into Spain, from whence he came back with difficulty, but to the great rejoicing of the whole people in general, who were much afflicted at his going thither. During this treaty the papists got many advantages of the king, to the prejudice of the protestant interest at home and abroad, and the hearts of all but the papists were very much saddened; and the people loath to lay the miscarriage of things at the king's own door, began to entertain a universal hatred of the Duke of Buckingham, raised from a knight's fourth son to that pitch of glory, and enjoying great possessions, acquired by the favour of the king, upon no merit but that of his beauty and his prostitution. The parliament had drawn up a charge against him, and though the king seemed to protect

him, yet knowing the fearfulness of his nature, and doubting his constancy, it was believed he added some help to an ague that killed that king; however the king died, and the duke continued in the favour of the next succeeding as of the deceased prince; whereupon one, not unaptly, says of him, "he seemed as an unhappy exhalation, drawn up from the earth, not only to cloud the setting, but the rising sun."

The face of the court was much changed in the change of the king, for King Charles was temperate, chaste, and serious; so that the fools and bawds, mimics and catamites, of the former court, grew out of fashion; and the nobility and courtiers, who did not quite abandon their debaucheries, had yet that reverence to the king as to retire into corners to practise them. Men of learning and ingenuity in all arts were in esteem, and received encouragement from the king, who was a most excellent judge and a great lover of paintings, carvings, gravings, and many other ingenuities, less offensive than the bawdry and profane abusive wit which was the only exercise of the other court. But, as in the primitive times, it is observed that the best emperors were some of them stirred up by Satan to be the bitterest persecutors of the church, so this king was a worse encroacher upon the civil and spiritual liberties of his people by far than his father. He married a papist, a French lady, of a haughty spirit, and a great wit and beauty, to whom he became a most uxorious husband. By this means the court was replenished with papists, and many who hoped to advance themselves by the change, turned to that religion. All the papists in the kingdom were favoured, and, by the king's example, matched with the best families; and the puritans were more than ever discountenanced and persecuted, insomuch that many of them chose to abandon their native country, and leave their dearest relations, to retire into any foreign soil or plantation, where they might, amidst all outward inconveniences, enjoy the free exercise of God's worship. Such as could not flee were tormented in the bishops' courts, fined, whipped, imprisoned, and suffered to enjoy no rest, so that death was better than life to them; and notwithstanding their patient sufferance of all these things, yet was not the king satisfied till the whole land was reduced to perfect slavery. The example of the French king was propounded to him, and he thought himself no monarch so long as his will was confined to the bounds of any law; but knowing that the people of England were not pliable to an arbitrary rule, he plotted to subdue them to his yoke by a foreign force, and till he could effect it, made no conscience of granting anything to the people, which he resolved should not oblige him longer than it served his turn; for he was a prince that had nothing of faith or truth, justice or generosity, in him. He was the most obstinate person in his self-will that ever was, and so bent upon being an absolute, uncontrollable sovereign, that he was resolved either to be such a king or none. His firm adherence to prelacy was not for conscience of one religion more than another, for it was his principle that an honest man might be saved in any profession; but he had a mistaken principle that kingly government in the state could not stand without episcopal government in the church; and, therefore, as the bishops flattered him with preaching up his sovereign prerogative, and inveighing against the Puritans as factious and disloyal, so he protected them in their pomp and pride, and insolent practices against the godly and sober people of the land.

The protestants abroad were all looked upon as Puritans, and their interests, instead of being protected, sadly betrayed; and all the flower of the English gentry were lost in an ill-managed expedition to the Isle of Rhé, under pretence of helping them, but so ordered that it proved the loss of Rochelle, the strong fort and best defence of all the protestants in France. Those in Germany were no less neglected in all treaties, although his own sister and her children were so highly concerned. The whole people were sadly grieved at these misgovernments, and, loath to impute them to the king, cast all the odium upon the Duke of Buckingham, whom at length a discontented person stabbed, believing he did God and his country good service by it. All the kingdom, except the duke's own dependents and kindred, rejoiced in the death of the duke; but they found little cause, for after it the king still persisted in his design of enslaving them, and found other ministers ready to serve his self-willed ambition, such as were Noy, his attorney-general, who set on foot that hateful tax of ship-money, and many more illegal exactions; and ten of the judges, who perverted judgment in the cause of those who refused the illegal imposition. Besides these, and a great rascally company of flatterers and projectors, there were all the corrupted, tottering bishops, and others of the proud, profane clergy of the land, who by their insolencies, grown odious to the people, bent their strong endeavours to disaffect the prince to his honest, godly subjects, and to get a pretence of power from him, to afflict those who would not submit to their insolent dominion. But there were two above all the rest, who led the van of the king's evil counsellors, and these were Laud, archbishop of Canterbury, a fellow of mean extraction and arrogant pride, and the Earl of Strafford, who as much outstripped all the rest in favour as he did in abilities, being a man of deep policy, stern resolution, and ambitious zeal to keep up the glory of his own greatness. In the beginning of the king's reign, this man had been a strong asserter of the liberties of the people, among whom he had gained himself an honourable reputation, and was dreadful to the court party; who thereupon strewed snares in his way, and when they found a breach at his ambition, his soul was that way entered and captivated. But above all these the king had another instigator of his own violent purpose, more powerful than all the rest, and that was the queen, who, grown out of her childhood, began to turn her mind from those vain extravagancies she lived in at first, to that which did less become her, and was more fatal to the kingdom; which is never in any place happy where the hands which were made only for distaffs affect the management of sceptres. — If any one object the fresh example of Queen Elizabeth, let them remember that the felicity of her reign was the effect of her submission to her masculine and wise counsellors; but wherever male princes are so effeminate as to suffer women of foreign birth and different religions to intermeddle with the affairs of State, it is always found to produce sad desolations; and it hath been observed that a French queen never brought any happiness to England. This lady being by her priests affected with the meritoriousness of advancing her own religion, whose principle it is to subvert all other, applied that way her great wit and parts, and the power her haughty spirit kept over her husband, who was enslaved in his affection only to her, though she had no more passion for him than what served to promote her designs. Those brought her into a very good correspondence with the archbishop and his prelatical crew, both joining in the cruel design of rooting the godly out of the land. The foolish protestants were meditating reconciliations with the church of Rome, who embraced them as far as they would go, carrying them in hand, as if there had been a possibility of bringing such a thing to pass; meanwhile they carried on their design by them, and had so ripened it, that nothing but the mercy of God prevented the utter subversion of protestantism in the three kingdoms. — But how much soever their designs were framed in the dark, God revealed them to his servants, and most miraculously ordered providences for their preservation.

The English People Seduced into Rebellion

THOMAS HOBBES

Born in the year of the Armada, Hobbes spent most of his life as a scholar, in the country houses of aristocratic patrons, especially successive Earls of Devonshire, or on European tours with them. He was a keen student of physics and mathematics, and his books on philosophy, law, and politics can be regarded as an attempt to apply scientific method, as he understood it, to those subjects. His most famous book, *Leviathan*, appeared in 1651. *Behemoth* was written in 1668, though not openly published until after his death in 1679. It is in the form of a dialogue; but the two characters cooperate in amplifying the discussion, rather than engaging in genuine controversy.

A. Truly, I think if the King had had money, he might have had soldiers enough in England. For there were very few of the common people that cared much for either of the causes, but would have taken any side for pay or plunder. But the King's treasury was very low, and his enemies, that pretended the people's ease from taxes and other specious things, had the command of the purses of the city of London and of most cities and corporate towns in England, and of many particular persons besides.

B. But how came the people to be so

From Thomas Hobbes, *Behemoth: the History of the Causes of the Civil Wars in England, and of the counsels and artifices by which they were carried on from the year 1640 to the year 1660*, in *The English Works of Thomas Hobbes*, ed. Sir William Molesworth, 6 vols. (London, 1840), Vol. VI, pp. 166–9, 213, 233, 236–7.

corrupted? And what kind of people were they that did so seduce them?

A. The seducers were of divers sorts: One sort were ministers; ministers, as they called themselves, of Christ; and sometimes, in their sermons to the people, God's ambassadors; pretending to have a right from God to govern every one his parish, and their assembly the whole nation.

Secondly, there were a very great number, though not comparable to the other, which notwithstanding that the Pope's power in England, both temporal and ecclesiastical, had been by Act of Parliament abolished, did still retain a belief that we ought to be governed by the Pope, whom they pretended to be the vicar of Christ, and in the right of Christ, to be the governor of all Christian people. And these were known by the name of Papists; as the ministers I mentioned before, were commonly called Presbyterians.

Thirdly, there were not a few, who in the beginning of the troubles were not discovered, but shortly after declared themselves for a liberty in religion, and those of different opinions from one another. Some of them, because they would have all congregations free and independent upon one another, were called Independents. Others that held baptism to infants, and such as understood not into what they were baptized, to be ineffectual, were called therefore Anabaptists. Others that held that Christ's kingdom was at this time to begin upon the earth, were called Fifth-monarchy-men; besides divers other sects, as Quakers, Adamites, &c., whose names and peculiar doctrines I do not well remember. And these were the enemies which arose against his Majesty from the private interpretation of Scripture, exposed to every man's scanning in his mother-tongue.

Fourthly, there were an exceeding great number of men of the better sort, that had been so educated, as that in their youth having read the books written by famous men of the ancient Grecian and Roman commonwealths concerning their polity and great actions; in which books the popular government was extolled by that glorious name of liberty, and monarchy disgraced by the name of tyranny; they became thereby in love with their forms of government. And out of these men were chosen the greatest part of the House of Commons, or if they were not the greatest part, yet by advantage of their eloquence, were always able to sway the rest.

Fifthly, the city of London and other great towns of trade, having in admiration the prosperity of the Low Countries after they had revolted from their monarch, the King of Spain, were inclined to think that the like change of government here, would to them produce the like prosperity.

Sixthly, there were a very great number that had either wasted their fortunes, or thought them too mean for the good parts they thought were in themselves; and more there were, that had able bodies, but saw no means how honestly to get their bread. These longed for a war, and hoped to maintain themselves hereafter by the lucky choosing of a party to side with, and consequently did for the most part serve under them that had the greatest plenty of money.

Lastly, the people in general were so ignorant of their duty, as that not one perhaps of ten thousand knew what right any man had to command him, or what necessity there was of King or Commonwealth, for which he was to part with his money against his will; but thought himself to be so much master of whatsoever he possessed, that it could not be taken from him upon any pretence of common safety, without his consent. King, they thought, was but a title of the highest honour, which gentleman, knight, baron, earl, duke, were but steps to ascend to, with the help of riches; they had no rule of equity, but precedents and custom; and he was thought wisest and fittest to be chosen for a Parliament, that was most averse to the granting of subsidies or other public payments.

A. The universities have been to this nation, as the wooden horse was to the Trojans.

B. For such curious questions in divinity

are first started in the Universities, and so are all those politic questions concerning the rights of civil and ecclesiastical government; and there they are furnished with arguments for liberty out of the works of Aristotle, Plato, Cicero, Seneca, and out of the histories of Rome and Greece, for their disputations against the necessary power of their sovereigns. Therefore I despair of any lasting peace among ourselves, till the Universities here shall bend and direct their studies to the settling of it, that is, to the teaching of absolute obedience to the laws of the King and to his public edicts under the Great Seal of England.

A. The core of the rebellion, as you have seen by this, and read of other rebellions, are the Universities; which nevertheless are not to be cast away, but to be better disciplined: that is to say, that the politics there taught be much to be, as true politics should be, such as are fit to make men know, that it is their duty to obey all laws whatsoever that shall by the authority of the King be enacted, till by the same authority they shall be repealed; such as are fit to make men understand, that the civil laws are God's laws, as they that make them are by God appointed to make them; and to make men know, that the people and the Church are one thing, and have but one head, the King; and that no man has title to govern under him, that has it not from him; that the King owes his crown to God only, and to no man, ecclesiastic or other; and that the religion they teach there, be a quiet waiting for the coming again of our blessed Saviour, and in the mean time a resolution to obey the King's laws, which also are God's laws; to injure no man, to be in charity with all men, to cherish the poor and sick, and to live soberly and free from scandal; without mingling our religion with points of natural philosophy, as freedom of the will, incorporeal substance, everlasting nows, ubiquities, hypostases, which the people understand not, nor will ever care for. When the Universities shall be thus disciplined, there will come out of them, from time to time, well-principled preachers, and they that are now ill-principled, from time to time fall away.

A Moderate Puritan Looks at the Extreme Policies of Sinful Men

RICHARD BAXTER

Born in 1615, Baxter was a minister in the Church of England from 1638; and after working mainly at Kidderminster in Worcestershire—though also spending some time as a chaplain in the Parliamentary armies—he became a professing Dissenter only in 1662. Although he must be called a Puritan, and although he engaged in frequent controversies, his primary concern was always with preaching and pastoral work, and his ideal was a universal Church which would include all true Christians. In his view, those who claimed exclusive righteousness, or argued fanatically for a single form of church organization, were the real sectaries and separatists, not the honest men troubled in conscience and seeking truth. Much persecuted in his later years, but, despite illness, a prolific author to the last, Baxter died in 1691. The *Reliquiae Baxterianae* was completed in manuscript about 1685, first published in 1696, and for many years was best known in Edmund Calamy's *Abridgment* of 1702.

IT is of very great moment here to understand the quality of the persons which adhered to the king and to the parliament, with their reasons.

A great part of the Lords forsook the parliament, and so did many of the House of Commons, and came to the king; but that was, for the most of them, after Edgehill fight, when the king was at Oxford. A very great part of the knights and gentlemen of England in the several counties (who were not parliament-men) adhered to the king. . . . And most of the tenants of these gentlemen, and also most of the poorest of the people, whom the other call the rabble, did follow the gentry and were for the king.

On the parliament's side were (besides themselves) the smaller part (as some thought) of the gentry in most of the counties, and the greatest part of the tradesmen and freeholders and the middle sort of men, especially in those corporations and countries which depend on clothing and such manufactures. . . .

But though it must be confessed that the public safety and liberty wrought very much with most, especially with the nobility and gentry who adhered to the parliament, yet was it principally the differences about religious matter that filled up the parliament's armies and put the resolution and valour into their soldiers, which carried them on in another manner than mercenary soldiers are carried on. Not that the matter of bishops or no bishops was the main thing (for thousands that wished for good bishops were on the parliament's side), though many called it *bellum episcopale* (and with the Scots that was a greater part of the controversy). But the generality of the people through the land (I say not *all*, or *every one*) who were then called Puritans, precisians, religious persons, that used to talk of God, and heaven, and Scripture, and holiness . . . I say, the

From the book *Autobiography* (1696). Everyman's Library. Reprinted by permission of J. M. Dent and E. P. Dutton & Co., Inc., pp. 34–5, 36–7.

main body of this sort of men, both preachers and people, adhered to the parliament. And on the other side, the gentry that were not so precise and strict against an oath, or gaming, or plays, or drinking, nor troubled themselves so much about the matters of God and the world to come, and the ministers and people that were for the King's Book, for dancing and recreations on the Lord's-days, and those that made not so great a matter of every sin, but went to church and heard Common Prayer, and were glad to hear a sermon which lashed the Puritans. . . .

If you ask how this came to pass, it requireth a longer answer than I think fit here to give; but, briefly, actions spring from natural dispositions and interest. There is somewhat in the nature of all worldly men which maketh them earnestly desirous of riches and honours in the world. . . . Yet conscience must be quieted and reputation preserved, which can neither of them be done without some religion. Therefore such a religion is necessary to such as is consistent with a worldly mind, which outside-formality, lip-service and hypocrisy is, but seriousness, sincerity and spirituality is not.

On the other side, there is that in the new nature of a spiritual believer which inclineth him to things above, and causeth him to look at worldly grandeur and riches as things more dangerous than desirable; and he is dead to the world, and the world to him, by the Cross of Christ. . . . And the laws of Christ, to which they are so devoted, are of such a stream as cannot suit with carnal interest. . . .

And thus the interest of the diocesans and of the profane and ignorant sort of people were unhappily twisted together in England. . . .

And abundance of the ignorant sort of the country, who were civil, did flock to the parliament, and filled up their armies afterward, merely because they heard men *swear* for the Common Prayer and bishops, and heard others *pray* that were against them; and because they heard the king's soldiers with horrid oaths abuse the name of God, and saw them live in debauchery, and the parliament's soldiers flock to sermons and talking of religion, and praying and singing psalms together on their guards. And all the sober men that I was acquainted with, who were against the parliament, were wont to say, "The king hath the better cause, but the parliament hath the better men." . . .

The king professed to fight for the subjects' liberties, the laws of the land, and the Protestant religion. The parliament professed the same, and all their commissions were granted as "for king and parliament," for the parliament professed that the separation of the king from the parliament could not be without a destruction of the government, and that the dividers were the destroyers and enemies to the State, and if the soldiers asked each other at any surprise or meeting, "Who are you for?" those on the king's side said, "For the king," and the others said, "For king and parliament." . . .

For my own part I freely confess that I was not judicious enough in politics and law to decide this controversy which so many lawyers and wise men differed in. And I freely confess that, being astonished at the Irish massacre, and persuaded fully both of the parliament's good endeavours for reformation and of their real danger, my judgment of the main cause much swayed my judgment in the matter of the wars. . . . And the consideration of the quality of the parties that sided for each cause in the countries did greatly work with me, and more than it should have done. . . .

I make no doubt but both parties were to blame (as it commonly falleth out in most wars and contentions), and I will not be he that shall justify either of them. I doubt not but the headiness and rashness of the younger unexperienced sort of religious people made many parliament men and ministers overgo themselves to keep pace with those hotspurs. . . . And as the secretaries increased so did this insolence increase. I have myself been in London when they have on Lord's-days stood at the church doors while the Common Prayer was reading, saying, "We must stay till he is out of his pottage." . . .

But I then thought that, whosoever was faulty, the people's liberties and safety could not be forfeited. And I thought that all the subjects were not guilty of all the faults of king or parliament when they defended them; yea, that if both their causes had been bad as against each other, yet that the subjects should adhere to that party which most secured the welfare of the nation, and might defend the land under their conduct, without owning all their cause . . . I was then so zealous that I thought it a great sin for men that were able to defend their country to be neuters; and I have been tempted since to think that I was a more competent judge upon the place when all things were before our eyes than I am in the review of those days and actions so many years after, when distance disadvantageth the apprehension. . . . But I confess for my part I have not such

censorious thoughts of those that then were neuters as formerly I have had: for he that either thinketh both sides raised an unlawful war, or that could not tell which (if either) was in the right, might well be excused if he defended neither.

I was always satisfied that the dividers of the king and parliament were the traitors, whoever they were; and that the division tended to the dissolution of the government. . . .

But matters that wars and blood are any way concerned in are so great and tenderly to be handled that I profess to the world that I dare not, I will not justify anything that others or myself have done of any such consequence. But though I never hurt the person of any man, yet I resolve to pray daily and earnestly to God that he will reveal to me whatever I have done amiss, and not suffer me through ignorance to be impenitent, and would forgive me both my known and unknown sins, and cleanse this land from the guilt of blood.

PART III: TEN VARIATIONS: SOME CONTRIBUTIONS OF MODERN SCHOLARSHIP

The Gentry Take the Power to Which Their Economic Success Entitles Them

RICHARD H. TAWNEY

R. H. Tawney (born 1880) has been a prominent writer on Socialism and a pioneer of adult education in Britain, as well as a leading economic historian. For many years he was Professor at London University. Most of his scholarly work has been on the Tudor and early Stuart periods.

THE facts were plain enough. The ruin of famous families by personal extravagance and political ineptitude; the decline in the position of the yeomanry towards the turn of the century, when long leases fell in; the loss, not only of revenue, but of authority, by the monarchy, as Crown lands melted; the mounting fortunes of the residuary legatee, a gentry whose aggregate income was put even in 1600 at some three times that of peers, bishops, deans and chapters, and richer yeomen together, and who steadily gathered into their hands estates slipping from the grasp of peasant, nobility, Church and Crown alike — such movements and their consequences were visible to all. Not only a precocious economist like Thomas Wilson the younger, the nephew of Elizabeth's Secretary of State, but men of greater eminence; Bacon; Cranfield; Selden; the shifty, but not unintelligent, Goodman; those artists in crying stinking fish, the

Venetian embassy in London; Coke, most amiable and most futile of secretaries of state, who begs Buckingham, of all people, to save Crown lands from the spoiler — wrote footnotes on the same theme.

The man who saw deepest into the moral of it all was primarily neither a theorist nor a politician, though he had the gifts of both. He was a great man of action, perhaps the greatest of his age. The doctrine that political stability depends on the maintenance of that Balance of Property, which was later to become a term of art, was not, in essence, novel. It was implicit in the conception of society as an organism, requiring the maintenance of a due proportion between its different members, which was part of the medieval legacy. But it is one thing to repeat a formula, another to apply it. Raleigh's dialogue, composed, it seems, in 1615, just after the central crisis of James' reign, was the first attempt to state the relevance of that conception to the

From R. H. Tawney, "The Rise of the Gentry, 1558–1640," *Economic History Review*, Vol. XI (1941), pp. 5–10, 10–13, 14–19, 23–25, 26–27, 28, 35–37. Reprinted by permission of the Editors of *Economic History Review*.

changing circumstances of his day, and to deduce from it the need, not for mere conservatism, but for reform. The argument with which his country gentleman confutes the noble parasite is no abstract disquisition on constitutional formalities. It is a deduction from social history. The centre of social gravity has shifted; political power is shifting with it. The Earl who could once put a thousand horse into the field cannot now put twenty-five; if the greatest lord lifts a finger, he will be locked up by the next constable. The commons to-day command most of the wealth, and all the weapons. It is they, not the heirs of the feudal past, who hold the keys of the future. It is with them; with their natural leaders, the gentry; with the House of Commons, which is their organ, that the monarchy, if it is wise, will hasten to make its peace.

These hints of political deductions from the fact of social change must not now detain us. In considering the character of that change itself, the right point of departure is that which Raleigh suggests. To speak of the transition from a feudal to a bourgeois society is to decline upon a *cliché*. But a process difficult to epitomise in less hackneyed terms has left deep marks on the social systems of most parts of Europe. What a contemporary described in 1600 as the conversion of "a gentry addicted to war" into "good husbands," who "knew as well how to improve their lands to the uttermost as the farmer or countryman," may reasonably be regarded as an insular species of the same genus.

It was a precocious species, which later, when its survival was assured, was to be the admiration of foreigners, but which for long found few imitators; nor was it accomplished without anguish. The movement passed through the three familiar stages of breakdown, reconstruction and stabilisation. If one aspect of the first phase consisted in the political and legal reforms by which the Tudor State consolidated its power, another aspect was economic. Jolted sharply by the great depreciation; then squeezed by its masters to find the means

for new styles in fashion and display; then pulled by expanding markets, when expedients adopted to stave off catastrophe were discovered, once systematised, to pay dividends beyond hope, agrarian society was everywhere under strain. The ability of nature to cause confusion with her silver is greatly inferior, as we now know, to that of human art; and, in view of the dimensions of the movement, the lamentations provoked by it seem to-day overdone. But, in judging the effects of this most un-revolutionary of monetary revolutions, three truisms must be remembered. It broke on a world which had known within living memory something like a currency famine. The society which experienced it was crossed by lines of petrifaction, which make modern rigidities seem elastic. Except for brief intervals, the movement was continuous, on the Continent for some three generations, in England for nearly four. The wave of rising prices struck the dyke of customary obligations, static burdens, customary dues; rebounded; struck again; and then either broke it, or carved new channels which turned its flank.

More than one country had known a dreadful interlude, when anarchy was not remote. In most it was discovered, when the worst was over, that the land system which came out of the crisis was not that which had gone into it. The key, as usual, was finance. The items comprising the landowner's revenue change their relative importance. The value of all customary and non-commercial payments tumbles down; that of the more elastic sources of income increases. Some groups can adapt themselves to the new tensions and opportunities; others cannot. The former rise; the latter sink. Examples of both are to be found in every stratum of society. There are grounds, nevertheless, for thinking that what Professor Bloch has called *la crise des fortunes seigneuriales* was felt more acutely, and surmounted with greater difficulty, by the heirs of ancient wealth, with its complex and dispersed interests, and large public responsibilities, than by men of humbler position or more recent eminence. Contemporaries noted the turn of the wheel in their superb prose. "How many noble families have there been whose memory is utterly abolished! How many flourishing houses have we seen which oblivion hath now obfuscated. . . . Time doth diminish and consume all." But time was not the chief destroyer.

Such a family, inheriting great estates, often inherited trouble. Its standards of expenditure were those of one age, its income that of another. "Port" — the display becoming in a great position — was a point of honour; who would wish to be thought, like Lord Dencourt, to "live like a hog"? "What by reason," wrote a close observer, "of their magnificence and waste in expense, and what by reason of a desire to advance and make great their own families," the life of a considerable part of the aristocracy was apt to offer an example of what a modern economist has called "conspicuous waste." Other regalities might have gone; what remained, and, indeed, increased, was a regal ostentation. The overheads of the great landowner — a great establishment, and often more than one; troops of servants and retainers; stables fit for a regiment of cavalry; endless hospitality to neighbours and national notabilities; visits to court, at once ruinous and unavoidable; litigation descending, like an heirloom, from generation to generation — had always been enormous. Now, on the top of these traditional liabilities, came the demands of a new world of luxury and fashion. With the fortunes resulting from inflation and booming trade all standards are rising. London, rapidly advancing in financial and commercial importance, with a court that under James is a lottery of unearned fortunes, exercises a stronger pull. Town houses increase in number; visits to the capital are spun out; residential quarters are developed; to the delight of dress-makers, something like a season begins to emerge. Culture has demands to which homage must be paid. New and more costly styles of building; the maintenance of a troop of needy scholars

and poets; collections of pictures; here and there — an extreme case — the avenues of posturing nudities which Bacon saluted at Arundel with ironical dismay — "the resurrection of the dead!" — all have their votaries. Public duties, in some cases, complete what private prodigality has begun. They yielded some pickings; but, under Elizabeth and her two successors, more than one bearer of a famous name was brought near to ruin by the crowning catastrophe of a useful career.

So towering a superstructure required broad foundations. Too often they were lacking. The wealth of some of the nobility, and especially of the older families, was not infrequently more spectacular than substantial. It was locked up in frozen assets — immobilised in sumptuous appurtenances, at once splendid and unrealisable. More important, the whole structure and organisation of their estates was often of a kind, which, once a pillar of the social system, was now obsolescent. Side by side with more lucrative possessions, their properties included majestic, but unremunerative, franchises — hundreds, boroughs, fairs and markets; a multitude of knights' fees, all honour and no profit; free-holds created in an age when falling, not rising, prices had been the great landowners' problem, and fixed rents were an insurance; hundreds of prickly copyholds, whose occupants pocketed an unearned increment while the real income of their landlord fell. What was the use, a disconsolate peer expostulated with the Queen, of pretending to relieve his necessities by the gift of a manor whose tenants were protected by law against an increase in rents, and by custom against an increase in fines? That cheerless condition was to be expected in properties which Elizabeth thought suitable for presents; but it was not, unfortunately, confined to them. The administrative machine which controlled a great estate had some of the vices of a miniature State department. It was cumbrous, conservative, difficult to divert from its traditional routine to new and speculative enterprises. The very magnitude and wide dispersal of the interests concerned — property of a dozen different kinds in a dozen different counties — made drastic reconstruction a formidable business, which it needed an exceptional personality to force through. It is not surprising that inherited opulence should sometimes have lacked the initiative to launch it.

Such difficulties confronted all conservative landowners, both peers and commoners, in proportion to the magnitude of their commitments and the rigidity of their incomes. The most that can be said is that the former usually carried more sail than the latter, and found it, when the wind changed, more difficult to tack.

The materials for generalisation have hardly yet been put together; but to say that many noble families — though not they alone — encountered, in the two generations before the Civil War, a financial crisis is probably not an over-statement. The fate of the conservative aristocrat was, in fact, an unhappy one. Reduced to living "like a rich beggar, in perpetual want," he sees his influence, popularity, and property all melt together. Some, like Lord Howard of Effingham and the Earl of Sussex, part with their estates to their creditors, or sell outlying portions to save the remainder. Some resort to half-obsolete claims on their tenants, with which, as a Lancashire landlord remarked, the victims comply, "if not for love, then for fear"; claims resembling, in their pedantic and exasperating legality, those most criticised in the Crown, but which — so merciful is history to the victors — are commonly ignored in the case of private landowners. Some, like the Berkeleys, do both. The sixth earl, for whom his admiring biographer — a lover of honorific titles — could find no more appropriate name than Lord Henry the Harmless, combined with the style and establishment of a medieval potentate the sporting tastes of a country gentleman; periodic plunges into the world of fashion in London; the maintenance of a *salon* as a concession to culture; and an heirloom in the shape of a lawsuit, which when he inherited it had already lasted a century, and which in 1609, four years before his death, he steered at last, with cries of self-congratulation, to a disastrous victory. While continuing to manage his Gloucestershire estates with a conservatism as agreeable to his tenants as it was fatal to himself, he sinks ever deeper into debt to tradesmen, to scriveners, to merchant-bankers; sells land outside the county to the value of £60,000; and ends his life in a maze of financial expedients, charged with a slightly exotic odour, as of the Seine rather than the Severn — collecting an aid from his freeholders to knight his eldest son, releasing his customary tenants from irksome obligations that had elsewhere long vanished, and raising a benevolence to pay for the ruinous results of his triumph as a litigant. Other landowners again — Lord Compton, Lord Noel, Lord Willoughby, the Earl of Holderness — restore their fortunes by marrying City money. Others, with a pull in the right quarter, plant themselves on the preposterous pension list of the Crown, angle — an odious business — for "concealed lands," or intrigue, with a kind of amateurish greed, for patents and monopolies.

Whether their embarrassments were increasing it is impossible to say; some debts, it is fair to remember, represented reproductive expenditure on developments and improvements. But soundings, wherever taken, show much water in the hold. The correspondence of Burleigh, in the last decade of Elizabeth, reads like the report of a receiver in bankruptcy to the nobility and gentry. A few years later, when, with the opening of the great boom which began in 1606, things should have been better, Cranfield, no financial leviathan, had a score of them in his books, while, to judge by stray references, Hicks the silk-man and banker — later Lord Campden — and Herriott, the goldsmith, may well have had more. Rubens, no stranger to the costly futility of courts, still retained sufficient naïveté to lift his eyebrows at the orgy of extravagance and peculation — "business, public and private, sold cash down, over the counter" —

which distinguished that of James. Clarendon's account of the notabilities of his day is a catalogue of splendid spendthrifts. When, in 1642, all went into the melting-pot, the debts owed to the City by Royalists alone were put, in a financial memorandum, at not less than £2,000,000. Of the commercial magnates who, a few years later, scrambled for confiscated estates, not a few were creditors entering on properties long mortgaged to them. It was discovered, not for the last time, that as a method of fore-closure war was cheaper than litigation.

For, if the new world had its victims, it had also its conquerors. That "the wanton bringing up and ignorance of the nobility force the prince to advance new men that can serve, which . . . subvert the noble houses to have their rooms themselves," had been noted with uneasiness in the early years of Elizabeth, when suggestions were considered for redressing the balance. Half a century later, the consequences of the movement were visible to all, and there could be no question of reversing it. "The age was one," writes Miss Wake in her account of Northamptonshire under James, "which had recently seen the rise of the solid middle class of lesser landowning gentry on the ruins of the ancient aristocracy. The families were few which . . . managed to survive the turbulent end of the middle ages. . . . Many of the knights and squires belonged to families of local and extraneous origin who had made money early in the previous century by the law, trade, or sheep-farming." That picture is true of more counties than one. The conditions which depressed some incomes inflated others; and, while one group of landowners bumped heavily along the bottom, another, which was quicker to catch the tide when it turned, was floated to fortune. The process of readjustment was complex; but two broad movements can be observed, affecting respectively the techniques of land-management and the ownership of landed property.

The situation confronting the landed classes in the half-century before the Civil War resembled in miniature that of 1850–70. Not only were prices rising, but, with the progress of internal unification, the development of specialised semi-industrial areas, and the growth of urban markets, demand was expanding. The advice to put estate management on a business footing was, in such circumstances, sound; but not everyone could take it, and not all who could would. Then, as now, rationalisation might look easy on paper, but was, in fact, no simple matter. Then, as now, therefore, what appeared at first sight a mere pedestrian improvement in methods of administration set in motion, as it developed, subtle social changes. It was to be expected that men with the resources and ambition to play the part of pioneers should gain at the expense of groups, whether below them or above, less qualified by means and traditions to adapt themselves to a new climate. The well-to-do yeoman, the *kulak* of the day, might maintain, or even improve, his position; but the extension of demesne farms, the upward movement of rents and fines, and encroachments on commons, combined in parts of the country to tilt the scales against the humbler peasants. To that chapter of the story, whose local diversities still remain to be worked out, but of which the outlines are known, must be added another, of which historians have said less, but by which contemporaries were impressed. There was a struggle for survival, not only between large landowners and small, but between different categories of the former.

It was primarily a struggle between economies of different types, which corresponded more closely with regional peculiarities than with social divisions. There are plenty of gentry who stagnate or go downhill. It would be easy to find noble landowners who move with the times, and make the most of their properties; the sheep-farming of Lord Spencer; the enclosures of Lords Brudenell, Huntingdon and Saye and Sele; the coal-mines of the Earl of Northumberland and the Earl of Wemyss; above all the grandiose reconstruction carried through by the Russells, are cases in point. The smaller the part, nevertheless, played by passive property, as compared with active enterprise, the larger the opportunities of rising; and the increased rewards to be reaped by the improving landlord favoured classes still ascending the ladder compared with those already at the summit. The charms of established wealth might be represented by an Earl of Newcastle, with a rent-roll of £22,000, or an Earl of Pembroke, with the ninety-three manors, four boroughs and estates scattered over ten counties from Middlesex to Yorkshire, which gave him, at his death in 1630, the reputation of one of the richest peers in England. But, when experiment and innovation were the order of the day, the cards were in other hands. They were all on the side of the enterprising country gentleman.

Professor Kosminsky has described the owners of "small and medium-sized estates" in the thirteenth century as "all people less intimately involved in the economic system of feudalism, and early subject to capitalist transformation." It is the representatives of much the same indeterminate middle class, with interests large enough to offer a secure base for manoeuvre, but not so large as to be top-heavy, who, three centuries later, are quickest, when the wind shifts, to trim their sails. Such a man was not tempted by great possessions into the somnolence of the *rentier;* was less loaded than most noble landowners with heavy overhead charges in the shape of great establishments; did his work for himself, instead of relying on a cumbrous machine to do it for him; owned, in short, his property, instead of being owned by it. Usually, unless one of the minority of active administrators, he was freer from public duties in his county, and more immune to the blandishments of London. The problem confronting him, if he undertook reconstruction or development, was of manageable dimensions. It demanded practical experience of farming, common sense, attention to detail, not the rarer gifts of the business strategist.

Under the pressure of an environment in motion, several types emerge. Some strike no roots; others survive and become fixed. There is the gentleman farmer, leasing land, till he makes money, without owning it, and not infrequently — since the thing is his profession — running several farms at once. There is the man who works his land as a commercial undertaking — a John Toke in Kent, buying Welsh and Scottish runts to finish on Romney marsh for the London market; a Robert Loder in Berkshire, all piety and profits; a Sir Thomas Tresham in Northamptonshire, selling everything, from rabbits supplied on contract to a poulterer in Gracechurch Street, to wool to the value of £1,000 a year, whose dual role as a leader of the Catholic cause in England and the most hated encloser in his much disturbed county is a point on the side of those who dismiss as a mare's nest the alleged affinities of economic and religious radicalism; a Sir John Wynn in North Wales, cattle breeder, tribal chieftain, land-grabber, scholar, and prospector for minerals unknown to science, with the vanity of a savage and the credulity of his beloved alchemists, whose dealings with his tenants were too much for his own class, and cost him his seat on the Council of Wales. There are families like the Pelhams and Twysdens, living mainly on rents, but doing on the side a useful trade in grain, hops, wool and iron in local markets and in London. Each type has its own idiosyncrasies, but none is in land for its health. All watch markets closely; buy and sell in bulk; compare the costs and yields of different crops; charge the rent, when custom allows, which a farm will stand; keep careful accounts. Mr. Fussell's description of one of them — "before all things a business man" — is true of all.

It was agricultural capitalists of this type who were making the pace, and to whom the future belonged. Nor, if land supplied the base from which they started, were their interests confined to it. The lament that "it is impossible for the mere country gentleman ever to grow rich and raise his house, he must have some other profession," was uttered at a moment when pessimism was pardonable, and was too pessimistic. It is true, however, that many of the class, whether of necessity or by choice, were up to the eyes in other branches of business. Naturally they turned first to the industries native to their own districts — iron in Sussex and the Forest of Dean; tin in Cornwall; lead in Derbyshire and North Wales; coal in Nottinghamshire, Durham and North-umberland; textiles in a dozen counties. But their business connections were not merely local. The habit of investment was spreading rapidly among the upper classes, and the starry host of notabilities, who lent lustre to the Virginia and East India Companies, contributed less to its development than did the web woven by the humbler ventures of hundreds of obscure squires. Some of them, too, held shares in those much advertised undertakings. More had relations in the City, and sent their sons into business. An increasing number — for the current did not run only one way — had been in business themselves.

"See," wrote Cobden to Bright, "how every successful trader buys an estate!" The remark might have been made with equal truth under James I. The movement from trade into land had long been an old story. Each successive generation made its bow to the proprieties by affecting surprise at it. It was not so long, indeed, since a states-man, alarmed at the crumbling of the social pyramid, had proposed to shore it up, by fixing a legal maximum to the real property which vulgar persons, like mere merchants, might buy. Thirty years later that pose had worn thin. The Government of the first two Stuarts continued, on a more majestic scale, the Elizabethan policy of turning Crown estates into cash. So far from depre-cating the acquisition of land by the busi-ness world, it threw land at its head. It was not surprising that a successful merchant, who had made his pile in trade, should prefer to the risks of commerce the decorous stability of what was regarded as a gilt-edged investment. By the middle years of James, if not, indeed, earlier, it is difficult to find a prominent London capitalist who is not also a substantial landowner; even such dubious cosmopolitans as Van Lore and Burlamachi, like Pallavicino before them, feel obliged to astonish the natives by setting up as country gentlemen. For-tunes made in law went the same way. Whether it is true or not, as was alleged, that leading barristers were making, in the later years of Elizabeth, £20,000 to £30,000 a year, there was general agreement that their emoluments were not trifling. Their profession had taught them what, properly handled, land could be made to yield; naturally, they used their knowledge. Pop-ham, who speculated heavily in Crown lands; Ellesmere, who left his son £12,000 a year; the odious, but indispensable, Coke, were all substantial landowners; the last, indeed, with his fifty odd manors, was well up in the first flight. In the twenties, the inroads of the London plutocracy on the home counties gave rise to complaints; and what was true of the neighbourhood of London was hardly less true of the environs of other growing cities, for example Bristol. In such conditions, the social categories used to distinguish the landed and trading classes, which in France and Germany remained terms with a legal significance, lost in England any claim to precision which they may once have possessed. The landowner living on the profits and rents of commercial farming, and the merchant or banker who was also a landowner, rep-resented, not two classes, but one. Patrician and *parvenu* both owed their ascent to causes of the same order. Judged by the source of their incomes, both were equally *bourgeois*.

The advance of the classes representing a more business-like agriculture was accom-panied by a second movement, which at once reflected its influence and consolidated its results. That movement was the height-ened rapidity with which land was chang-ing hands. The land-market deals in a form of capital, and, in many societies, the most important form. The article which it han-dles is not merely a commodity, but an instrument of social prestige and political power. It is most active, therefore, when a rise in incomes swells the surplus for investment, and when wealth, in addition to increasing, is passing into new hands. Commercial expansion, industrial progress, discovery and invention, but also financial recklessness, revolution and war, have at different times set the wheel spinning with heightened speed. In the age of Elizabeth and her two successors, economic and political conditions combined to mobilise real property, while the hostility of the courts to entails gave both forces free play. The former, apart from occasional severe depressions, acted continuously, and with increasing force, to augment the demand for it. The latter, by periodically bringing fresh blocks of land into the market, supplied recurrent opportunities for profitable speculation.

Periodical redistributions of land by acts of public policy, to the gain or loss now of this class, now of that, are not the astonishing departure from pre-established harmonies which they appear to their victims. In one form or another, they are a recurrent feature of European history, whose repeated appearance lends colour to the view which sees in them, not an accident, but the prelude to a new era. The decorous story of England is no exception to that rule. In the century and a half between the Reformation and the Restoration, such a redistribution took place on a scale not seen since the Conquest. There were two immense confiscations, the result of revolution and civil war, and a steady alienation, under financial duress, of estates formerly used to provide a revenue for public purposes.

The opening act of the drama is not here in place. But the story which had begun with the Dissolution [of the Monasteries by Henry VIII] had not ended with it. Like taxation, the fruits of confiscation do not always rest where they first light. It is an error to suppose that, when James skipped happily on to his throne of thorns, the results of that great transaction were already ancient history Property producing a gross income equal to about half the then yield of the customs had been cut adrift from its moorings, and added to the acreage available for acquisition by influence or enterprise. When the first fever of speculation was over, it had continued to float from hand to hand in the ordinary way of business, coming at intervals to anchor only again to resume its exciting voyages. Nor had the Crown's interest in the matter ceased with the mere act of confiscation and the sales which followed it. For one thing, though it had disposed within a decade of the greater part of the spoils, those which it retained remained substantial. For another, part of the land with which it had parted had not been sold outright, but had been leased for terms of years, and ultimately returned to it. In the third place, part of that which it sold came back to it later through escheats and confiscations. Two generations later, therefore, it still owned, as a result of the Dissolution, a great mass of property, which could be leased, mortgaged or sold, and which, when the Court of Augmentations was wound up in 1554, had continued to be administered by the Augmentations office of the Exchequer. A vast deal in Chantry lands brought temporary relief to the financial embarrassments of the early years of James. His son was disposing of monastic estates within a decade of the Long Parliament.

The continued redistribution of monastic property in the century following the Reformation was as momentous, therefore, as that which accompanied it. The transference to lay hands of part of the land owned by bishops and by deans and chapters — "their wings . . . well clipt of late by courtiers and noblemen, and some quite cut away" — has been studied in detail only during the Interregnum, but the statements of contemporaries suggest that the scale on which it took place under Elizabeth was not inconsiderable. Nor was it only ecclesiastical property which came into the market in large blocks. Few rulers have acted more remorselessly than the early Tudors on the maxim that the foundations of political authority are economic. They had made the augmentation of the royal demesnes one of the key-stones of their policy. They had enjoyed, as a consequence, not only a large revenue from land, but the extensive economic patronage which great estates conferred, and had been powerful as Kings partly because unrivalled as landowners. A shrewd foreigner remarked, as he watched in the next century the headlong plunge downhill of the Crown finances, that the Stuarts were on the way to be overshadowed in wealth by their subjects before they were overthrown by them. There was some substance in the view, hinted more than once under James, that the New Monarchy was undermined by reversing in three generations the financial policy which had helped to establish it. Each of the three great crises of Elizabeth's reign carried its own block of Crown estates away; she sold in her forty-five years land to the value, in all, of some £817,000. Her two successors inherited the nemesis of living on capital, as well as of rising prices and their own characters. They sold in thirty years nearly twice as much. In spite of half-hearted attempts to tie his hands, alienations of property under James reached about £775,000, and those of Charles I, in the first decade of his reign, over £650,000. The estates remaining to the Crown, when the Long Parliament met, were still, of course, substantial; but how ruinously they had been dilapidated can be shown by a comparison. Between 1558 and 1635 Crown lands to the value of some £2,240,000 had been thrown on the market. When, in the crisis of the Civil War, the remains were swept together and put up to auction, the sum realised, it seems, was under £2,000,000.

The settlement of monastic estates into the hands of the most progressive element in rural society may be illustrated by the course of events in one small corner of the country. In Gloucestershire, Northamptonshire and Warwickshire about 317 manors, together with a mass of miscellaneous property — tithes, rectories and land in different places — appear to have changed hands at the Dissolution. Of the manors, which are more easily traced than the smaller acquisitions, between 250 and 260 passed into the ownership of individuals, the remainder being obtained by bishops, deans and chapters, colleges and other corporations. The nobility had done fairly, though not immoderately, well; twenty-six peers had acquired monastic property of some kind, and seventeen had secured just over forty manors. Crown officials, like Sadler and Kingston, the two largest grantees of Gloucestershire estates; big business, in the persons of Gresham, Sharington and Stump; and an ubiquitous group of professional speculators, had all got their share; while a number of smaller men picked up crumbs from the cake. The bulk of the property had gone, however, not to influential aliens, but to well-known local families. In Gloucestershire, the beneficiaries had included Chamberlains, Poynzs, Thynnes, Throckmortons, Tracies, Dennises, Porters, Comptons and Botelers; in Northamptonshire Montagues, Knightleys, Kirkhams, Cecils and Fermors; in Warwickshire Knightleys, Aglionbys and Throckmortons. Precision is impossible; but it is probably not an exaggeration to say that from one-half to two-thirds of the property acquired by individuals had passed to men of this type and to humbler members of the same class. In so far as there had been competition between national notabilities and tenacious local interests, local interests had won.

Their victory became steadily more decisive in the course of the next century. Compared with the adventurers who dealt in properties that they had never seen, the local gentry were a settled population confronting mere marauders. As the revolution receded, and its first turmoil died down, their strategic advantage — the advantage of a settled base — asserted itself with ever-increasing force. Political convulsions shook down the estates of one group of absentees; financial embarrassments sapped the staying-power of another. As each over-rigged vessel went on the rocks, the patient watchers on the shore brought home fresh flotsam from the wreck. Long after the last monk had died, they were adding to their abbey lands, and, if not admitted on the ground floor, became shareholders at one remove. . . . The general result in these counties, [Gloucestershire, Northamptonshire, and Warwickshire] . . . was that, of the forty odd manors which had gone to peers at the Reformation, those remaining to them two generations later numbered only six, while the remainder swelled the fortunes of rising middle-class families. Something between two-thirds and three-quarters of the manors secured by private persons had gone originally to the squirearchy. By the early years of the next century, the proportion in their hands was over nine-tenths. Thus the ultimate consequences of the Dissolution, if similar in kind to its immediate effects, were different in degree. In this part of England, at any rate, it did not so much endow an existing nobility, as lay the foundations of a new nobility to arise in the next century.

Mr. Russell Smith, in his interesting study of Harrington, has suggested that the thesis as to the political repercussion of changes in the distribution of landed property, which is the central doctrine of the *Oceana*, if partly inspired by a study of Roman history, derived its actuality from the English confiscations in Ireland under the Act of 1642 and the Diggers' movement in England. In reality, it was needless for Harrington to look so far afield as the first, or in spheres so humble as the second. In so far as he was in debt to previous writers, his master was Macchiavelli; but the process from which he generalised had been taking place beneath his eyes. His own relatives had been engaged in it.

Had he shared the modern taste for figures, he would have found little difficulty in supporting his doctrine by some casual scraps of statistical evidence. He would have observed, for example, had he taken as a sample some 3,300 manors in ten counties, that out of 730 held by the Crown and the peerage in 1561, some 430 had left them (if new creations are ignored) by 1640, while an additional 400 had been acquired by the gentry. He would have discovered that, as a consequence, the Crown, which in 1561 owned just one-tenth (9 per cent) of the total, owned in 1640 one-fiftieth (2 per cent); that the peers held one-eighth (12.6 per cent) at the first date, and (ignoring new creations) one-sixteenth (6.7 per cent) at the second; and that the share of the gentry had risen from two-thirds (67 per cent), when the period began, to four-fifths (80 per cent) at the end of it. His remarks on the social changes which caused the House of Commons "to raise that head which since hath been so high and formidable unto their princes that they have looked pale upon those assemblies," and his celebrated paradox, "Wherefore the dissolution of this Government caused the war, not the war the dissolution of this Government," were based on his argument as to the significance of a "balance" of property; and that argument took its point from his belief that in his own day the balance had been altered. To the sceptic who questioned its historical foundations, he would probably have replied — for he was an obstinate person — by inviting him either to submit rebutting evidence, or to agree that there was some *prima facie* reason, at least, for supposing that, in the counties in question, the landed property of the Crown had diminished under Parthenia, Morpheus and his successor by three-quarters (76 per cent), and that of the older nobility by approximately half (47.1 per cent), while that of the gentry had increased by not much less than one-fifth (17.8 per cent).

In reality, however, as far as this side of his doctrines were concerned, there were few sceptics to challenge him. To regard Harrington as an isolated doctrinaire is an error. In spite of its thin dress of fancy, his work was not a Utopia, but partly a social history, partly a programme based upon it. Contemporaries who abhorred the second were not indisposed to agree with the first, for it accorded with their own experience. The political effect of the transference of property appeared as obvious to authors on the right, like Sir Edward Walker, whose book appeared three years before the *Oceana*, as to Ludlow, to that formidable blue-stocking, Mrs. Hutchinson, and to Neville, on the left. If, in 1600, it could be said that the richer gentry had the incomes of an Earl, and in 1628 that the House of Commons could buy the House of Lords three times over, the argument advanced in some quarters in 1659 that, since the Peers, who once held two-thirds of the land, now held less than one-twelfth, the day for a House of Lords was passed, was not, perhaps, surprising. It overstated its case; but a case existed.

Poor and Discontented Gentry Rebel Against Established Institutions

HUGH R. TREVOR-ROPER

Regius Professor of Modern History at Oxford since 1957, H. R. Trevor-Roper (born 1914) published his first book, *Archbishop Laud*, in 1940. His military service led to a brilliant book in another field, *The Last Days of Hitler*. Since World War II, he has returned to his early Stuart specialization, though he writes short articles and reviews on many topics in periodicals for the general reader.

THE social interpretation of the Great Rebellion, or Puritan Revolution of 1640–60, is one of the most controversial subjects among English historians to-day. Not only conflicting, but entirely opposite and incompatible, views are held about it. But before considering these views, let me remind readers briefly of the course of events to which they apply.

The Great Rebellion began in 1640 with the summoning of the Long Parliament which, having forced Charles I to end his period of "personal rule," and having removed the ministers who had governed in his name, enacted a series of constitutional reforms. Unfortunately, the Parliament had just grounds for distrusting the King's good faith, and this distrust, combined with certain political accidents, led, in 1642, to Civil War. In order to win this war the Parliament was obliged, in 1645, to create a new army, and this new army soon became the instrument of a new party in the country. This new party, the party of the Independents, soon showed itself as a revolutionary party which made all previous politics obsolete: it overpowered the Parliament, executed the King, destroyed the monarchy, and set up, under Oliver Cromwell, a military regime which did not founder until after his death.

Now in the social interpretation of these events the crucial question is, who were these Independents? What social forces did they represent? What did they seek to do? And this is the question which has elicited the most various answers.

The classic answer, which has been

From Hugh R. Trevor-Roper, "The Social Causes of the Great Rebellion," in *Historical Essays* (London, 1957), pp. 195–205. Reprinted by permission of the author and of Harper Brothers.

underwritten by some of the most distinguished historians and promptly accepted as the orthodoxy of the Schools, is that of the doyen of English social and economic history, Professor R. H. Tawney. This view rests on three major premises. First, Tawney accepts, at least in some sense, the view of Max Weber that Puritanism was the ideology of capitalism, that "capitalism was the social counterpart of Calvinist theology." Secondly, he supposes that the period from 1540–1640 was a period, in England, of continuous economic advance by the "capitalist" and Puritan classes, who, with increasing prosperity, became increasingly resentful of the paternal restrictions imposed by the state. Thirdly, he supposes that the gentry was a force on the side of capitalism. The gentry, he argues, by introducing capitalist principles of land-management, became a rural branch of the bourgeoisie, a continuously "rising" class, unlike the aristocracy, who, being committed to obsolete methods, were rapidly declining into debt and ruin. On the basis of these premises, Tawney interprets the Great Rebellion as the last, violent episode of the victory of the prosperous, self-confident, impatient bourgeoisie over the old order, impoverished, anachronistic, but tenacious. According to this view, the crown and the aristocracy were a debtor class, the merchants and gentry a creditor class; and the Great Rebellion was a kind of forcible foreclosure of impatient *nouveau-riche* creditors on evasive aristocratic debtors: "It was discovered, not for the last time, that as a method of foreclosure war was cheaper than litigation."

Now this view, which of course I have greatly (but, I think, not unfairly) simplified, has recommended itself to a very wide range of historians. Roman Catholics, seeing Protestantism equated with capitalism by scholars, and capitalism turned into a word of abuse by socialists, have been quick to seize their advantage and declare that the Protestant Reformation in England is thus proved to have been "a rebellion of the rich against the poor," leading to all the ills

that modern socialists complain of. Marxist historians, declaring summarily that the equation of Puritanism with capitalism is one of "the irresistible conclusions of modern research," announce that the Puritan Revolution was the crucial victory in the world struggle of capitalism to burst its "feudal" bonds: it was "the decisive shift" from a generally feudal to a predominantly capitalist society. . . . Had the English revolution failed, as so many other revolutions in the seventeenth century failed, it is entirely possible that economic development might have been long retarded. As it was (they say) "the Revolution triumphed, with portentous results": the Puritan onslaught broke down the resistance of feudalism and by its success secured the victory of capitalism in the world. The army of Cromwell provided the shock-troops of the bourgeoisie.

Now my interpretation is very different from this view of the Tawney school. It could hardly fail to be, because I disagree fundamentally with all three of its major premises. First, I do not think that there is any exclusive connection between Puritanism and Capitalism: I find that the English Puritans included strong anti-capitalist forces, and that orthodox Calvinism, so far from being the ideology of the merchant classes in the seventeenth century, prevailed largely — in Protestant countries — among backwoods squires, as in Scotland and Gelderland. Secondly, whatever may be said of the period before 1590, I do not think that the years 1590–1640 were a period of growing general prosperity in Europe, or even in England (though certain special trades, centred in London, brought prosperity to certain great London merchants and, of course, government financiers). Thirdly, I do not think that the gentry were "rising" in that period: on the contrary, I find evidence of general decline among those whose income came solely or largely from land. In fact, I do not think that "capitalism" played any great part in the Revolution: the City of London was royalist and had to be drastically purged four times in order to keep it in line with the rebels, and the parliamentary boroughs, whose support to the opposition has been claimed as evidence of mercantile feeling, did not represent merchant feeling at all: they were "rotten boroughs" controlled by great magnates whose opposition was far from mercantile in character. Finally, I do not believe that the Revolution "triumphed with portentous results." I believe that it failed.

I shall not use space here in destructive argument. In this essay I propose to consider the social nature of the revolution by asking two questions of fact: first, what was the economic position of the gentry, who, since they dominated both Parliament and local government, were the essential social class in any parliamentary and national movement? and, secondly, what were the most insistent claims of the "Independents" who provided the revolutionary force in this movement? Fortunately, in the increasing quantity of local and family history, in the parliamentary records and vast pamphlet literature of the period, we have abundant evidence on which to attempt an answer to this question.

First, what was the economic state of the gentry? In my opinion, Tawney has misrepresented this problem by selecting, as instances of a general economic "rise of the gentry," only those families whose fortunes, in fact, can be shown to have come not from land but from office. Office-holders naturally owned land; but land was not the source of their wealth: it was not even necessarily an economic investment: it was a social asset — it may even have been an economic liability. If we wish to learn about the state of the gentry, we must not consider such office-holding gentry but the "mere gentry," "les pauvres gentilhommes," as Cardinal Richelieu called them, "dont le bien ne consiste qu'en fonds de terre." If we do this, I think we discover overwhelming evidence that such men, in England as in France, were in economic difficulty.

Wherever we look, it is the same. In North Wales, the gentry were all declaring themselves ruined. In Staffordshire, be-

tween 1600 and 1660, half the land was said to have been sold. It was out of the estates of decayed northern gentry that the Countess of Shrewsbury and Lord William Howard endowed the noble houses that they founded, and in 1614, when the first Earl of Cork wanted to establish his family in his home county, he was told that he could please himself "for half of Herefordshire is for sale." In the same year, "most of the ancientest gentlemen's houses" in Northamptonshire were declared "either divided, diminished or decayed." In the last few years, many good manors had been sold, but "not a gentleman of the county hath bought any, but strangers and they no inhabitants." In Nottinghamshire, in 1625, the sheriff reported that the resident gentry had been much diminished, bought out by strangers. The lands in Berkshire were likened to skittish horses which often threw their owners. Modern scholars have shown that the gentry of Devonshire were almost universally in debt in the 1630's, that those of Lincolnshire were almost all declining, and that, in Bedfordshire, Buckinghamshire and Northamptonshire, one family in three among them, between 1600 and 1640, was selling its land. Clearly the decline was not merely local: it was general, throughout England.

And who were the "strangers" who are named as thus buying up the decaying gentry? The Earl of Cork, the Countess of Shrewsbury, her son the Earl of Devonshire, Lord William Howard — officers and grandees of the court; Alderman Soame, Alderman Craven, Alderman Cokayne, Sir Thomas Middleton, Sir Arthur Ingram, Sir Baptist Hicks — great merchants and government financiers from the City of London. It is an oligarchy of metropolitan plutocrats, aldermen of London and courtiers of Whitehall, who are sucking the life out of the "mere gentry" and "decayed boroughs" of the provinces. For it is because boroughs are economically "decayed" that they become politically "rotten," and sell their independence to aristocratic patrons. Thriving towns, like Newcastle-upon-Tyne, linked to London by the coal trade, or Bristol, the port of Western trade, continue to elect their own representatives.

What were the gentry to do in such circumstances? In Spain, the impoverished *hidalgo* had a solution: *iglesia o casa real o mar,* office in Church or Court, or the sea. The English gentleman thought in the same terms. "It is impossible," wrote one of them, "for a mere country gentleman ever to grow rich or raise his house. He must have some other vocation with his inheritance, as to be a courtier, lawyer, merchant, or some other vocation. If he hath no other vocation, let him get a ship and judiciously manage her, or buy some auditor's place, or be vice-admiral in his county. By only following the plough he may keep his word and be upright, but will never increase his fortune. Sir John Oglander wrote this with his own blood, June the 25th, 1632." It was no accident that the first thirty years of the seventeenth century saw an unprecedented scramble for office, an unprecedented and rising market in office, a desire to make office hereditary, as in France; and that, in the 1630's, when the more parsimonious government of Charles I cut down the opportunities at court, there was an unprecedented emigration of the gentry to North America. Nor is it an accident that the gentry, who thus embarked on colonial schemes, were Puritans and became the leaders of the Independents. Puritan austerity was often the religion not of rich capitalists, saving to invest, but of poor gentry, saving to make ends meet, and morally disgusted at the ostentation and extravagance of a court from which they were excluded and which flourished at their expense. It was appropriate that the leader of these gentry, when they became revolutionary, should have been Oliver Cromwell — the representative of a former court family, now reduced to their lands and obliged, in his youth, to sell their great house in Huntingdonshire to a new family drawing its income from office and the law.

Thus the Great Rebellion, in my opinion, is not the clear-headed self-assertion of the rising bourgeoisie and gentry, but rather the blind protest of the depressed gentry. In the 1630's, incidental political factors increased this depression, and the radical gentry willingly supported the aristocratic politicians who sought, by parliamentary pressure, to bring the King back into the ancient constitutional ways. Unfortunately, these aristocratic leaders afterwards proved unable to contain their radical followers. Under the pressure of fear and civil war, the aristocratic leadership crumbled; and, in 1645, the Independents stood forth, mobilised, invincible, revolutionary, demanding satisfaction.

What were the demands of the Independents? Socially they are clear enough. They wanted independence from Court and City, the two swollen products of Tudor centralisation to which the provinces — the "mere gentry" and the "decayed boroughs" — had so long been sacrificed. They wanted decentralisation of government — the Cromwellian government would cut down the borough seats in Parliament and treble the county seats; decentralisation of religion — toleration instead of a centralised Anglican or Presbyterian Church; decentralisation of trade — that is to say, the break-up, not the formation of that national market which is essential to capitalism — "I thought," protested a West Country gentleman, "that long ere this we should have had trade dispersed all the nation over, but this City, it seems, must have all the trade"; decentralisation of law — local county registries, local courts; decentralisation of education — local schools, local universities. It was in the reign of the Independents that universities were projected in Wales and Cornwall, at York and Manchester, and a short-lived university founded in Durham. Socially, the Independent revolt was a revolt of the provinces against a century of Tudor centralisation: against that enslavement of the country by the Court and City to which the depressed gentry ascribed their present plight.

But what of their political claims? When we ask this question we soon find that they were entirely negative. The Independents knew what they hated. They hated the Court, with its office-holders, its lawyers, its pensioners, its monopolists, its archaic taxes; they hated the Lords, those great courtiers — he hoped, Cromwell once said, to live to see never a nobleman in England; they hated the centralised Church, which had tried, under Archbishop Laud, to rob them of their patronage and their tithes. They hated the all-absorbent City — "this nation," they said, "was falling into the rickets: the head bigger than the body." And, in their radical mood, they duly destroyed these things. They executed the King, abolished the House of Lords, sold up the Church, purged the City.

But what were their positive alternatives? They were not republicans, or whigs or mercantilists. A little "whig" republican group, which did obtain the leadership in Parliament for a time, was soon eliminated. The Independent gentry had no positive theories: one form of government, they said, was as good as another; they would really prefer to be governed than to govern, to be "tolerated" by a paternal government, under which they could prosper, than to exercise direct power, which they found too difficult. As to the form of that government — if pressed, they thought that "a government with something monarchical in it" was probably the best thing. On second thoughts, Lords were a good thing too: "we would keep up nobility"; and so was an established Church — they had never wanted to separate from the Anglican Church but only to live more comfortably in it than Archbishop Laud had allowed. The only thing that was *not* good was government by or for capitalists. Every aspect of Cromwell's rule aroused squeals of despair from the mercantile classes; but when they protested, he told them sharply to keep to their counting-houses. A whig champion of the merchant class really answered the theorists of the capitalist revolution, long before they had spoken, when he entitled his diatribe against the economic policy of the Protectorate "The World's Mistake in Oliver Cromwell."

In truth, the Independents did not know what they wanted in politics. As Cromwell himself once said: "none climbs so high as he who knows not whither he is going." Or rather, what they wanted was so vaguely envisaged that they could not think of any constitutional formula to achieve it. What they wanted was "a commonwealth." The conception of "the commonwealth," of an organic, almost a collectivist society, had been a commonplace under the Tudors and the great Tudor statesmen, Thomas Cromwell and Lord Burghley, and their social philosophers, "the Commonwealth men," had sought, however imperfectly, to realise it. But with the coming of the Stuarts, those feckless Scottish kings, this ideal had been rejected by a government of irresponsible courtiers and favourites and had been inherited instead by the Puritan opposition to government: an opposition not only inflamed by gentry grievances but also fired by a just indignation against feeble, bad and irresponsible government, the betrayal by selfish governors of "the honest part of the nation." Hence the cult, by the Puritans, not of new or mercantile or republican ideas, but of a vague, romanticised English monarchy such as they supposed had existed under the last sovereign of the old dynasty, "Queen Elizabeth of glorious memory." When the Independent Army reasserted itself and effortlessly drove out of power the little coterie of "whig" republicans who had usurped authority in its absence, the essential justification for that act was that the republican government thus overthrown was not, as it called itself, a "commonwealth," but "an oligarchy, detested by all men that love a commonwealth." And so Oliver Cromwell and his Independents replaced the policy of *laissez-faire* at home and mercantile aggression abroad against England's trade rivals, the Dutch, by an anachronistic revival of "Elizabethan" policy: paternal government, enforcement of poor laws and tillage laws, leadership of the "Protestant interest" in Europe, a protectorate over the Netherlands, a piratical war in the West Indies to tap the American treasure of Spain.

The Independent ideal was thus essentially an archaism. Unfortunately, the Independents could think of no institutions in which to crystallise and preserve such an archaism. Their philosopher, James Harrington, the author of *Oceana,* proposed a parliament of gentry holding office by rotation. That would prevent the rise of a privileged bureaucracy. More radical, Thomas Hobbes advocated the preservation of the old Tudor hierarchy and "degree" — which alone, according to the Tudor philosophers, prevented man's natural wickedness from destroying the commonwealth — by an open resort to naked, unsanctified power. Both Harrington and Hobbes conveniently ignored the existence of mercantile classes. But in fact even these desperate philosophies could not recreate that obsolete ideal. After a series of short-lived constitutional experiments, the Independents threw up the sponge and submitted again to the time-honoured rule of King, Lords, Commons and Established Church. Harrington died and was forgotten. Hobbes survived and was tolerated, in the new age, as a harmless old crank. The whole world of the Independents was rejected and became, in gay Restoration England, something of a joke. It is difficult to describe this as "success" or "triumph." "Success" by the Independents would have been a kind of decentralised anarchical gentry-republic, a Polish Diet. It is just as well that they failed.

And yet, protest our theorists, whatever the *nature* of the revolution, surely the *result* of it was a capitalist advance? If a new class had not come to political power, may it not nevertheless, behind the appearance of political continuity, have occupied the seats of social power? For, at the Restoration, one great change that had taken place was not reversed: the great transfer of land by enforced private sale.

Now of the purchasers of these lands, says the Marxist historian Archangelsky, fifty-one per cent were London merchants; and thus, says another scholar, the Restoration settlement was economically "a triumph for the 'new men' — men who may best be described . . . as business men who had thriven under the Commonwealth." But alas, even this conclusion cannot now be sustained. Recent research has shown that the "new men," of whom Marxist historians have made so much, were, to a very large extent, merely agents, buying back their lands for the old families, and that the land settlement of the Restoration passed through a royalist Parliament so easily because, in fact, the net effect of these sales had been insignificant. Socially, as politically, the Revolution had been a failure, and the history of England after 1660 was a continuation of its history before 1640. The Interregnum was merely an untidy interruption. The only permanent changes were a few constitutional changes that could have been, and sometimes had been, achieved by peaceful legislation, and certainly did not require civil war, revolution and military dictatorship.

Thus I conclude that the Great Rebellion was not a "capitalist" rising, nor did it "succeed" in any sense, nor in any way directly forward the advance of capitalism in England. It was the blind revolt of the gentry against the Court, of the provinces against the capital: the backwash against a century of administrative and economic centralisation. Since they were animated by passion, not by positive political ideas, and since they soon either lost by death, or overpowered and destroyed their political leaders, the radical gentry, when they were in power, found themselves without a policy. Ultimately, after a period of fumbling experiments, they gave up the effort, accepted back the old political system, and sank into political quietism. They might still grumble about Court and City; but, instead of arming themselves with radical ideas, they consoled themselves with conservative ideas: they became high-flying tories, preachers of non-resistance and divine right.

Thus, in my opinion, whatever results followed from the Great Rebellion followed not from its success but from its failure. The rebellion itself was a blind rebellion, which took place because a failure of political ability coincided with a general economic crisis. There were reformers; there were capitalists; there were political thinkers; and, had there been no rebellion of the gentry, these might well have achieved their aims by peaceful progress. But the rebellion of the gentry, a rebellion of mutinous, impoverished, backward-looking provincial squires, gave them no chance — at least until that rebellion had consumed itself and outlasted some of its causes. Perhaps *indirectly* the rebellion may have forwarded the undoubted change of mentality between the early and the late seventeenth century in England: by burning up both itself and its mental fuel, it may have cleared the way for the progress of new and very un-puritan ideas. But, equally, it may have impeded that progress for a generation. We cannot say. What we can say — or, at least, what I am prepared to say — is that it was not, in itself, a successful stage in the rise of the bourgeoisie. As in most revolutions, much of its momentum was self-generated; but in so far as it can be reduced to simple, fundamental terms, it was a protest, by the victims of a temporary general depression, against a privileged bureaucracy, a capitalist City.

The Wealthy Parliamentary Gentry — and the Reality of Ideology

J. H. HEXTER

Born in 1910, and educated at Cincinnati and Harvard, Hexter taught for years at Queens College, New York City. He is now professor at Washington University, St. Louis. In addition to his work on the seventeenth century, he is the author of an outstanding book on Thomas More's *Utopia*. In this article, Hexter launches a powerful attack on many of the assumptions—as well as some of the facts—in the long controversy about the role of the gentry in our period.

LET us examine these different kinds of evidence.

As to general statements by men of the times, alleged by Professor Tawney and Professor Trevor-Roper in support of their divergent conceptions, a little caution suggests itself. The human propensity to make a poor mouth knows no bounds of time or space. Consider, for example, the claim of penury put in by Sir Edward Montague on behalf of the county of Northampton in the reign of James I. The claim is cited by both Professor Tawney and Professor Trevor-Roper as evidence of the impoverishment of that sector of the landed class which the exigencies of their respective and opposed arguments require them to impoverish. The condition of the native Northamptonshire

From J. H. Hexter, "Storm over the Gentry," *Encounter*, May, 1958, pp. 23–4, 24–6, 26–7, 27–30, 31–4. Reprinted by permission of the Editors of *Encounter*. The whole essay is to be reprinted, early in 1961, by Longmans, Green, under the title, *Reappraisals in History*.

gentry may, of course, have been quite as parlous as Sir Edward's remarks indicate; but with only an *ipse dixit* to support his allegations, it seems pertinent to give some slight attention to the context of those allegations, to the circumstances and situation that elicited them. The observations are dated 1614, a year in which, Parliament having failed to pass a tax bill, the government was pressing the gentlemen of every county for a benevolence — a free offering. The observations are from a gentleman with a considerable estate in Northamptonshire. They are addressed to the Earl of Exeter, the Lord-Lieutenant of the county, and therefore the semi-official link between the county and the court. And they are headed, "Reasons to satisfy some that think Northamptonshire a rich county and underrated in subsidies and other charges. . . ." In courts of law, such a testimony from such a source is usually described as self-serving.

Moreover, the notion that one's own time is a brazen time in contrast to some good old golden age is common enough in every era. And writing at a later date, the historian can find support for his thesis — whatever it may be — among contemporaries, because those contemporaries had dramatically before their eyes, and had generalised from, the same sort of *particular* instances that the later historian has patiently dug out and generalised from.

Why individual cases can illustrate but cannot demonstrate either thesis is quite clear. The individual cases cited on both sides were in fact inherent in the structure of English society and polity in the period under consideration — and before and after. Surely, at any time a hundred and fifty years either way of 1600, *some* landed families, both noble and gentle, because of recklessness, extravagance, or failure to adjust to economic changes, had to sell land; *some* landed families, both noble and gentle, through good management and good marriages, were able to buy land; *some* families that owed a large increase in their fortunes to trade, or the practice of law, or office, or royal favour, were purchasing estates or adding to their land-holdings. All these things were happening between 1540 and 1640 too. That they were happening is all that the particular instances set forth by Tawney, Stone and Trevor-Roper demonstrate, and all they can demonstrate. In such circumstances, the significance of the individual instance for the theories depends on the validity of the general argument, not the other way about. So we "will have grounds more relative than this."

Professor Tawney provides such grounds in the form of statistics. His statistics are of two kinds: (1) casual statistics offhandedly dropped to lend artistic verisimilitude to large and bald assertions; (2) systematic statistics intended to provide a quantitative foundation for the general hypothesis that he is propounding. We shall consider Professor Tawney's use of both kinds of statistics in turn.

Professor Tawney has not always been aware of the pitfalls that some of his casual statistics conceal, and consequently he has not always alerted his readers to the dangers.

When we learn that fifty Royalists, whose confiscated estates in eight south-eastern counties the Commonwealth and Protectorate sold after 1650, were in debt to the tune of £140,000, the supposed £2,000,000 that Royalists owed in London seems plausible enough, and the notion of a general foreclosure on the Royalist aristocracy seems not far-fetched. But, alas, it turns out that fully four-fifths of the total debt of our fifty Royalist landowners were owed by just one man, the Earl of Cleveland. That truly "splendid spendthrift" was foreclosed right enough, properly sold up. His fate suggests two reflections. First, unless the security for his borrowings was remarkably good, we might want to withhold just one tear from the noble bankrupt in order to shed it over his bourgeois creditors. Second, a few such colossi of prodigality as the Earl of Cleveland would account for the whole of Royalist indebtedness in London and leave the rest of the cavaliers an astoundingly solvent lot. And when one considers that the average indebtedness of the forty-nine Royalists who were *not* the Earl of Cleveland was a mere £570 apiece, such a conclusion would seem plausible.

Nevertheless, not all the Royalists repurchased their estates. Only one-third of the confiscated parcels sold in eight south-eastern counties were bought back by their former owners — 34 out of 100. But when we break these figures down, we get an interesting slant on Professor Tawney's theory that the Revolution achieved the final liquidation of an unthrifty nobility and registered the triumph of the rising gentry. We omit the Earl of Craven, who thought he knew a cheaper way than buying it to get his land back. The rest of *the peers* in this group were the former owners of 24 confiscated properties. In 1656 the same peers were once more the owners of 23 *out of the 24 properties*. In this particular aspect of the process, the "foreclosure" of the "aristocracy" by civil war involved the loss of one life interest in a farm.

When we take away the properties of the peers from the total of confiscated Royalist properties in eight south-eastern counties, another curious fact emerges. Of the remaining properties, only fifteen per cent appear to have been repurchased by their former owners. Unless we assume what does not seem too probable, that those owners did not want to buy their property back, then it seems likely that most of them for lack of cash and lack of credit could not buy it back. Now these impecunious owners were rural landlords, lesser gentry; and it begins to look as if these out-of-pocket Royalist gentlemen constitute a sort of subversive fifth column of declining gentry sneaked by Professor Trevor-Roper into the south-east, the home territory of Professor Tawney's rising gentry. Except, of course, that it would seem according to Trevor-Roper's theory that, of all the mere gentry, the mere gentry of the Puritan south-east should have come up Independent, not Royalist at all.

The systematic statistics that Professor Tawney uses to support his general hypothesis concerning the rise of the gentry are provided by the counting of manors, 2,547 manors in 6⅓ counties. The count shows that the noble families which held a little more than 13 per cent of those manors in 1560 held a bare 6 per cent in 1640. The count also shows that the gentry, which in 1560 owned but two-thirds of the manors, eighty years later owned four-fifths of them.

Furthermore, the statistics[1] indicate that in 1560 about a quarter of the counted manors had belonged to men who each held ten or more of them, 57 per cent to men who held four manors or less. Whereas in 1640, less than one-sixth of the manors belonged to men who held ten or more of them, while men who held four or less owned 64 per cent of the manors involved.

But the statistics will not bear analysis. For (1) they have embedded in them a number of serious biases; (2) manors — the unit of counting — are anything but homogeneous; and (3) the contrast between aristocracy and gentry that the statistics are supposed to reveal involves an arbitrary and largely false taxonomic assumption.

First, let us look at the statistical evidence that is supposed to demonstrate the superior economic strategy of the small gentry. The basis of this evidence is a count of the manors held by men owning no more than four manors in 6⅓ counties. If all such men held no manors at all anywhere else, the inference drawn from this evidence might be of some interest. But 17th century landlords did not conform their holdings to the statistical convenience of 20th century economic historians. A very considerable number of gentlemen with no more than four manors in the 6⅓ sample counties owned manors in the remaining 33⅓ counties of England, in Wales, and in Ireland. Some of them, far from being small landowners, were very large landowners indeed.

[1] These figures of Professor Tawney's are in a footnote to *Economic History Review*, XI (1941), p. 33, and are not reproduced in the excerpt from "The Rise of the Gentry" in this book. [Editor's note]

And of course any assertion about the total number of manors held by small landowners becomes meaningless when we actually have no notion how many of the landowners so classified really were small.

Professor Tawney's estimate of a very heavy loss of manors by large landlords is open to a somewhat different criticism. The trouble in this instance is that one of the aristocratic large holders included in Professor Tawney's statistics was too aristocratic and too large. He was the King. Between 1540 and 1640 the Crown divested itself of vast chunks of land; this is one fact that Professor Tawney has established beyond all doubt. In his 6⅓ county sample, the Crown holding of nearly 250 manors dwindled to about 50 manors in 1640. *This whole loss Professor Tawney appears to have debited to the holders of ten or more manors.* When we remove the crown lands from consideration, the loss of the large holders, men who owned ten or more manors in the sample counties, drops from the 33 per cent that led Professor Tawney to consign them to bankruptcy, to ½ of 1 per cent, hardly a presage of impending economic catastrophe.

What then does account for the losses of the nobility and the gains of the gentry that Professor Tawney's other set of statistics seems to reveal? For one thing the "nobility" held fewer manors in 1640 than in 1560, because there were fewer "nobles" in 1640 than in 1560. For in his computations Professor Tawney classifies as noble only men who held peerages in 1560 and the inheritors of such peerages. But in 1640 one-third of such peerages were extinct, and extinct peers hold no manors at all. So some part of the loss of manors by the nobility, which Professor Tawney ascribes to economic causes, is due to normal demographic attrition. Another part is due to circumstances unique to the peculiar status of the peerage. Some of the land of peerage families goes to pay for the marriage settlements of daughters; some goes to provide for younger sons. When a peer dies without a son, the *peerage* usually passes to his male

heir, if there is one, but much of his *estate* may be divided among his heirs general. In the eight decades between 1560 and 1640 all these circumstances took their toll of the manors held by the successors in title to the men who were peers in 1560, and Professor Tawney's statistics register them all.

Now, dying without a son to inherit the family estate and making provision for daughters and younger sons out of such an estate are not among the special privileges of the peerage. They are the sort of things that happen to many an English gentleman, and they must have happened to many who were gentlemen in 1560, extinguishing those families or wearing down their holdings. But such losses scarcely ever show in Tawney's statistics as a loss to the gentry. They cannot show because *anyone but the inheritor of a peerage of 1560 who acquires the lost manors of the gentry is classified, merely in virtue of his acquisition, as gentry.* Professor Trevor-Roper rightly points out that while the group which Professor Tawney has classified as aristocracy "consists of a diminishing group of those families who happened to be noble at the beginning and still noble at the end of the period, his gentry consists both of the gentry who remained gentry throughout the period, and of those men who began as gentry and ended as peers, and of those who began as merchants, yeomen, or anything else, and ended as gentry. No wonder the gentry, thus calculated, appear to 'rise' at the expense of the peerage."

Economically, manors are not equivalent units like dollars or pounds or even bushels of wheat. They are incommensurate units of ownership like "blocks" of stock or the "properties" of present day real-estate parlance. There is a property, a 125 ft. by 40 ft. lot with a two-storey house on it, in darkest Queens in New York City: I own it. There is another property, a somewhat larger lot at 34th Street and 5th Avenue with the Empire State Building on it: someone else owns it. A statistical study of the trend in real-estate transactions in which these properties appeared as equivalent units might lead to conclusions a little askew. So may a study of the trend of real-estate transactions from 1560 to 1640 when manors are taken as units.

Nor are we quite at the end of our difficulties. In quest of a new rising rural middle class and an old declining aristocratic class to contrast one with another, Professor Tawney hit upon the gentry for the former role, the lay peerage for the latter. Professor Tawney's scheme of classification, his identification of the peerage with the aristocracy and the gentry with the middle class, renders *all* his statistical findings irrelevant to the theory that they are intended to support. For whether rising or not, the gentry did not stand to the peerage in the relation of a middle class to an aristocracy. Economically, gentry and peerage were of the *same* class — the class that ordinarily drew the larger part of its income from the exploitation of proprietary rights in land. Although in theory peerage conferred on its possessor a status higher than that enjoyed by holders of any lesser honour, a peer of recent vintage and slender substance confronted by a many-acred gentleman of ancient lineage might discover that the theory was devoid of significant practical consequences. Time eroded too many ancient noble fortunes, the royal whim conferred peerages on too many persons of slight stature to allow of any precise equation of peerage with prestige. Neither a distinctive economic class nor a clear-cut prestige group, peerage was a legal status constituted as a consequence of the past favour of English monarchs. Collectively, but not individually, the peers were the first gentlemen of England in honour and wealth, clearly distinct from the rest neither in source of livelihood nor way of life. So Professor Tawney's numerical evidence is erected on an error of classification — a statistical mirage reared on a taxonomic illusion.

Instead of statistics, Trevor-Roper offers us a brief but brilliant sketch of his conception of the role of the "mere" or declining gentry in the politics and society of England from the age of Elizabeth to the Restoration.

That this perdurable and undistinguished group was at large in England between 1540 and 1640 is evident. That its numbers may have been somewhat augmented and its collective temper somewhat exacerbated by the combined operations of adverse economic circumstances and Stuart indifference to their plight is quite probable. That various mere gentlemen had a hand in every attempted *coup d'état* from the rebellion of the Earl of Essex to the march of the New Model Army on London, Trevor-Roper has demonstrated beyond doubt. That after some of the mere gentry had stumbled towards power during the interregnum and staggered from ineptitude to ineptitude under the burden of responsibility, a few of them sought consolation in the pseudo-realistic Utopia of Harrington, is quite likely. So far, what Trevor-Roper has to say seems most plausible. But rather often he goes beyond these plausibilities to broad though somewhat vague assertions. There are, he seems to indicate, really only two kinds of gentry — the fat court gentry and the depressed country gentry. The Great Rebellion thus becomes "the rising of the poor country gentry against the office-holders." The Independents, who are mere gentry, convert the crisis of 1640 "from a series of political manoeuvres into civil war and social revolution." It is they "who more than any others made the Great Rebellion."

At this point the scope of Trevor-Roper's generalising brings one to an abrupt halt; for it certainly goes beyond the evidence. In the first place most of the Independents were *not* gentry, either rising or declining. And however well the policy of the Independents may have mirrored their psyche, most of the declining gentry were *not* Independents. The gentry of the North and West, regions that provided such superior facilities for going to pot on a stagnant rent roll, seem to have been predominantly Royalist. Moreover, a considerable number of the squires who sat in the Long Parliament, both Royalists and Roundheads, were in quite comfortable circumstances. They were neither overstuffed court gentry, nor bankrupt mere gentry, but substantial, fully solvent, country gentry. Dividing the English landlords of the century before the Great Rebellion between rising court and declining country gentry is a little like dividing the participants in the French Revolution between aristocrats and *enragés*: it leaves out an awful lot of important people and makes it unduly hard to explain what actually happened.

Recent investigation seems to show that, without the benefit of either demesne farming or court favour, from the 1580's on, the large landlords may have been doing very well for themselves. Around the 1580's the land market began to boom, and it seems to have continued to boom for the next half century. In those roaring days the annual rental on some estates climbed to a third of what those estates had sold for a few decades earlier. Incomes from new takings doubled, quadrupled, sometimes went up eight-fold. Landlords who had earlier gone into debt to hold their estates now reaped a golden harvest. So did those who had sold outlying manors to concentrate their holdings into manageable blocks and to pay the costs of "improving" their principal estates, that is, of renegotiating the terms of tenancy on them. The landed magnate rich enough and prudent enough to pay the high overhead costs of old-fashioned, tight-reined estate management now had his rewards. This reward was not within the reach of smaller men who could not afford the expensive personnel that such management demanded. In this period of rising land values the more industrious and alert among the lesser gentry most likely enjoyed those small gains that were commensurate with their small holdings. But on the whole, a general increase in land values is likely to be most profitable in gross to the men who have the most land to profit from — that is, to the very segment of the landed class which both Tawney and Trevor-Roper have consigned to economic debility. The neglect or misplacement of

this segment by both writers leaves an unfortunate gap in their respective reconstructions of the socio-economic configuration of the English countryside between 1540 and 1660.

It leaves a political gap even more unfortunate. For these large landholders were men who provided the realm with the more important part of that "self-government at the king's command" which one writer considers the most significant distinguishing trait of the English polity. They were the deputy-lieutenants. They were the sheriffs. They were the justices of the peace. They were the commissioners in the counties to look into the myriad of things that the Tudors and early Stuarts thought needed looking into, and the commissioners to do in the counties the myriad of things that the Tudors and early Stuarts thought needed to be done. Such charges did not fall in the main to "mere" gentry, out of sorts, out of pocket, down at the heels. And although rising courtiers, rich in lands, might appear on the rolls in the commission of the peace, and on other local commissions, they could not afford to give much time to county matters: rising at court required above all a man's regular presence at court. It was to the local magnates, "men of port and worship" in their neighbourhood, that the pains and the prestige of local authority fell. And from before the accession of Elizabeth I it was these same men who came to Parliament from the counties and boroughs to make up the larger part of the membership of the House of Commons. The majority of local magnates seems to have increased right up to 1640, so that in the House of Commons of the Long Parliament all other groups appear as auxiliaries — mere Balearic slingers and Nubian cavalry — to the close-packed legions of the rich, much-landed gentry.

The close relation between the rich country gentry and the lower house of Parliament may help to explain a rather puzzling feature common to Tawney's and Trevor-Roper's account of the century before 1640. This is their well-nigh sphinx-like silence with respect to the role of the House of Commons during that century. Such a silence is inevitably somewhat perplexing to historians who, having approached the era from the constitutional side, have learned to think of the doings in the House of Commons as matters of some consequence in the days of the Stuarts. Yet the silence is natural enough. For whether the lesser landlords were rising with Tawney or declining with Trevor-Roper, they cut but a small figure in the affairs of Parliament before the Great Rebellion; and to Trevor-Roper's rising court gentry in the days of the early Stuarts, the House was not at home. The men our two writers have selected as protagonists simply did not occupy what historians have long deemed the centre of the stage in the political drama of the epoch.

Not only does the personnel of the early Stuart House of Commons fall outside the orbit in which Professors Tawney and Trevor-Roper ordinarily move; its political behaviour does not reflect what they — and, I fear, a great many others — believe the purposes and aims of a powerful politico-social group must be. In short, from the accession of Elizabeth I to the summoning of the Long Parliament, the rich country gentlemen who fill the House of Commons make no consistent or concerted effort to win permanent control and direction of the government. They do not claim or seek for the House of Commons a sovereign power over the King. They do not even claim that the King-in-Parliament is always superior to the King-out-of-Parliament. Their whole line of conduct is sure to be confusing to the point of unintelligibility to those who approach it with a simplicist conception of politics in mind. Tawney's picture of a power-hungry rural middle class moving inexorably towards domination over the ruins of a feudalism that the middle class itself destroyed seems peculiarly irrelevant to many of the utterances and actions of the rich country gentry in

the Parliament of the early Stuarts. To the members of the House of Commons in those days, "power" was a dirty word. So much was this so, that in matters in which to us the issue of power seems to have been unmistakably and inescapably posed, in matters, too, in which they had the country strongly on their side, the Commons persistently encumbered their action by intricate arguments and manoeuvres to transform issues of present power into claims of ancient and traditional right. They did this despite the fact that making a case in law often presented well-nigh insuperable difficulties. They neither talked nor acted like would-be rulers of the realm. Trevor-Roper's presentation of the House as the politically befuddled and obtuse head of a rout of angry, hard-pressed yokels is not very convincing either. For the leaders of the early Stuart Parliaments were an unusually well-educated group of men; and it is hard to believe that the members who so neatly, quickly, and effectively won the initiative in Parliament from the King were a gang of inept political Calibans.

To construct an adequate account of the varied political attitudes and aims of the rich country gentlemen who crowded into the Parliaments of the first Elizabeth, James, and Charles is beyond the scope and purpose of this paper and beyond the ability of its author. It may be worth while, however, to make a few obvious points in the hope of clearing away some of the more permanent obstacles to such an account. In the first place it is *not* true that a political or social group occupying a strategic position in the power structure will necessarily and always use that position to seek supreme political power for itself. Such a group may instead seek to define certain terms and conditions within which the existing supreme authority shall be exercised. In the second place, it is *not* true that all the purposes and interests which such a group tries to protect and advance are necessarily and always peculiar to that group. Some of those purposes and interests it may share jointly with other segments of the society; some, indeed, may be interests common to all the ruled as against the supreme ruling power. The way of wisdom, therefore, may not always be to seek for a particular interest behind any action of a powerful group nor to concentrate one's attention entirely on those actions in which the particular interest of the group is clearly evident.

These strictures are readily applicable to the House of Commons in the early 17th century. If we do not confine our attention to the affairs in which the rich country gentry of the day had an obvious particular interest — for example, wardships, purveyance, distraint of knighthood, enclosure, breach of forest law, concealed lands — we may note that the House of Commons was also concerned with such matters of joint and common interest to many Englishmen as the independence of the judiciary, the survival of representative institutions, freedom from arbitrary arrest, defence against arbitrary exactions by the state, and preservation of the rule of law. If we incline to regard the latter common interests as of greater importance than the former particular ones, we may fortify our conviction from the record of the 17th century House of Commons: for on the face of that record, it is clear enough that the rich country gentry who dominated the House of Commons shared our conviction. The duration and intensity of their discussion of issues of common concern considerably exceed the time and effort they devoted to dealing with their particular group interest.

Finally, if we do not insist that the 17th century House of Commons aimed at supreme power, we can spare ourselves explaining away the inordinate amount of backing and filling the House engaged in when it found itself confronted with the problem of power. We hardly need be surprised that the House showed itself indecisive and uncertain in the face of the question of the nature and locus of supreme authority in the realm, for that, after all, is the toughest of all problems of power. But the same rich country gentlemen who did not know what they wanted for themselves in the way of power knew very well what they did not want for the King in the way of power, and throughout the 17th century they showed remarkable skill both in country charges and in the House of Commons in seeing to it that the King did not get what they did not want him to have.

Supposing the analysis, presented above, of the data put in evidence by Tawney and Trevor-Roper to be well-founded, what then is the present standing of the controversy over the gentry? With respect to Trevor-Roper's part in it, in fairness we need to add a little to what we have previously had to say. We have hitherto been more concerned to criticise what appear to be errors than to render due praise to merit. Yet in Trevor-Roper's studies there is substantial merit to praise.

(1) A very considerable part of Trevor-Roper's contribution to the controversy has taken the form of an all-out assault on the interpretive structures reared by Professor Tawney and Mr. Stone. Up to now we have paid little of the tribute due to his magnificent if terrifying work of destruction.

(2) In insisting on the court-against-country element in the crisis of the 17th century and in giving substantial content to the otherwise evanescent conception of "Court," Trevor-Roper has performed a service of inestimable benefit to historians of the period.

(3) He has provided us with a study of a social group, the declining gentry, that historians of the period from 1540 to 1640 have hitherto neglected. He has discovered some of the forces that may have moulded the outlook of that group and has related the political conduct of some of the declining gentry to the outlook he ascribes to them. A trifle exalted, perhaps, by his discovery, he has claimed for the declining gentry of the 17th century a somewhat larger historical role than a calmer and

fuller analysis is likely to attribute to them — a sin, possibly, but a venial one.

It is otherwise with the theory espoused by Professor Tawney and Mr. Stone. Mr. Stone has recently written:

It is now something of a commonplace that the collapse of the *ancien régime* in 1640 was an event that must be related to a shift in the social balance, the transfer of a section of the national income away from the Crown, some of the Peerage, and the Episcopacy to the middle class of gentry, officials, and lawyers that took place in the preceding century.

It does seem indeed that the hypothesis of Professor Tawney and Mr. Stone is on the verge of enshrinement in the pantheon of historical commonplaces. What else can be said for it? Only that it is an interesting theory, that the evidence thus far adduced in its support is unconvincing, and that the data underlying that evidence is in large part misleading, ambiguous, irrelevant, or merely erroneous.

When historians as able as Professor Tawney and Professor Trevor-Roper pile on their evidence a burden of hypothesis heavier than that evidence can sustain, we may suspect that their judgment has been clouded by over-addiction to some general conception of the historical process. Professor Tawney is sufficiently explicit about the incentive for his fascinating redrafting of the historical picture of the gentry and for his singular view of their social orientation. The English gentry, that is to say, must be transfigured into the bourgeoisie to maintain the view that the rise of the bourgeoisie is the indispensable framework for almost a millennium of history.

The general conception that dominates Trevor-Roper's studies also finds the source of human action in the circumambient economic configuration. But for him the motor of history is not the great impersonal secular movements of economic change; it is simpler than that. Groups of men in similar market situations are driven to common action and a common outlook by the similar way in which the same events impinge on their identical economic interests. This is a kind of economic determinism; but it is the motives of groups, not — as in Professor Tawney's case — the pattern of history, that are economically determined.

On a slightly broader view, Trevor-Roper's protagonists and antagonists, his court Rosencranzes and Guildensterns, his country Shallows and Silences, do not seem quite of a stature to bear the historical burden he imposes upon them. Perhaps that is why he pares down the burden, reducing that fairly magnificent upheaval, the Puritan Revolution, to the dimensions of a foolish farce that could conceivably have been brought off by the lowgrade louts and sharpers who people his stage. In the squalid setting of this farce there is not enough room for William Chillingworth or Richard Baxter, for Edward Coke or Francis Bacon, for Thomas Wentworth or Oliver Cromwell, for John Selden, or John Lilburne, or John Hampden, or John Pym, or John Milton. In such a setting, men of such stature and many others like them would poke their heads right up through the ceiling; for with all their limitations they were men who stood high enough to see a little beyond the deedbox and the dinner table. Somehow, without these men I find the age of the Puritan Revolution a little dull. What is worse, without some understanding of what such men stood for in their own eyes and in the eyes of others I find that age not very intelligible.

We are still left with the problem that started Tawney on his quest. The problem may be defined in the following fashion. In medieval England, leadership of the "country" opposition to the policies of the Crown had always rested in the hands of the great lords, the territorial magnates. Throughout the decades of growing estrangement from royal policy that preceded the Great Rebellion, however, it was not the great lords who organised and directed the "country" opposition. In this crucial period of English history the burden of leading that opposition was borne mainly by a cluster of prosperous country gentlemen and successful country lawyers who sat in the House of Commons. Why at this particular juncture did the "country" find its leadership in social strata beneath the top? Why among the gentry rather than among the nobility? Why instead of hearing of the Earl of This or Baron That do we mostly hear of Sir Edward Coke and Sir Thomas Wentworth and Sir John Eliot, of Edward Dering and Edward Hyde, of John Hampden and John Pym, of the Five Knights and the Five Members?

Cleared of subsequent and extraneous complications, this is the problem that Tawney faced. In the sense set forth in the preceding paragraph, the rise of the gentry is not a hypothesis to be verified; it is a simple fact, a fact that requires explanation. . When Professor Tawney sought to explain the fact of the rise of the gentry, he assumed that the solution of his problem must be sought in some transformation in the *economic* situation of the gentry on the one hand, of the great magnates on the other — in the economic rise of the gentry, the economic decline of the "aristocracy." We have learned to look with some reservations on the evidence which Tawney adduced in support of his solution to the problem of the gentry. But the reservations are directed towards the *solution,* not towards the *problem.* The problem remains — real enough and challenging enough. And we cannot turn to Trevor-Roper for a solution. For him the problem does not exist. He divides effective activity, before the outbreak of the Civil War, between Royalist aristocrats who are "in" and "Presbyterian" aristocrats who are "out," leaving the mere gentry who, like Huck Finn's father, are just "agin the guv'ment," in a posture of ineffectual intransigence. This procedure really involves turning our back on the problem and acting as if it were not there.

If we reject Professor Tawney's own solution of the problem that lay at the beginning of his quest, do we have any clue as to the direction in which we might seek a solution? We do have such a clue, I believe; and oddly enough, Professor Tawney provides it. Among the quotations from contemporaries on which he relies — quotations which, it seems to me, do little to support his argument — there are several that point clearly to a line of enquiry that he disregards. Now these men seem to be saying much the same thing about the noble magnates; but what they are saying is not that the nobles are bankrupt, or even much poorer than they used to be. They are saying very emphatically that *the magnates do not directly control arms and men as they once did,* that the old relation between high status or great landed wealth and a great military following no longer subsists. On the face of it, these observations direct our attention not to the economy but to the organisation of armed forces. And if we follow their leading, we discover that in the century and a half between Henry VI and the death of Elizabeth there was indeed a transformation in the structure of England's military reserve. In the middle of the 15th century, the larger part of the battle-ready military reserve was made up of the retinues of the magnates. Besides the magnates' tenantry, lesser landlords bound themselves to the great men of the realm by "writing, oath, or promise"; in return, they often received from their lord a sort of uniform, his livery, which they wore as a sign of their ·clientage. They also usually received a money fee which conjoined them to the lord's band of retained men, his retinue. Most fee'd retainers were bound to come at the call of their lord, prepared to fight under his command and in his quarrels. In return, besides fee and livery, the magnate gave his follower "goodlordship," which might mean anything from using his influence at court to gain for his retainer some office that the latter coveted, to overawing a jury that would otherwise take a strait-laced, provincial, and unsympathetic view of his retainer's propensity to trespass or homicide.

At the end of the 16th century the bare form of the retaining system survived; but it was a mere shell, a feeble shadow of its former self. The squirearchy no longer rose in arms at the behest of the great lords, although for show they might ride about the country in some personage's train. In 1628 Parliament repealed almost every statute passed during the preceding two hundred and fifty years to regulate, control, or suppress the evil practices that flourished under the protection of the retaining system. In so doing Parliament did not aim, by giving it legal sanction, to reinvigorate a living institution but only to provide a decent and honourable interment for an institution long since dead.

With its cement of retaining fatally weakened, the whole framework of good-lordship, from which the 15th century magnate derived his power, loosened up. To have the goodwill of the neighbouring great lord was no doubt still advantageous, but at no major peril lesser landlords could get along without it. Consequently the gentry of the Tudor period acted with greater independence than their predecessors in the days of Lancaster and York.

In the years of crisis in the early 17th century no serried arrays of gentle henchmen of noble houses took their political orders from the heads of those houses. Having lost their vocation for commanding retinues of armed squires, the magnates had not yet found their vocation for commanding solid phalanxes of borough members sitting in Parliament for the rotten and pocket boroughs that the magnates controlled. The result was a power vacuum in England during the very years when a concurrence of fiscal, constitutional, political, and religious grievances evoked widespread opposition to the Crown and made it necessary for the opposition to achieve some measure of concerted action. Into the vacuum created by the temporary incapacity of the magnates poured the country gentry — not the brisk, hard-bitten small gentry of Professor Tawney nor yet the mouldy, flea-bitten mere gentry of Professor Trevor-Roper, but the rich, well-educated knights and squires who sat in the Parliaments of James I and Charles I. There they do not seem to have formed tight, well-knit "interests" as their successors a few decades later were to do. Rather, they — especially those among them who came back to one Parliament after another — formed inchoate groupings, loose "connexions," occasionally joined but not, as far as I can judge, controlled by one or other opposition peer. It was in such invertebrate groupings that the rich gentry of England organised themselves to oppose the activities of the King in the most severe constitutional crisis in English history. It is not an accident that when at last the opposition rallied under one "overmighty" subject, that subject for the first time in the annals of England was not a great territorial magnate but a substantial squire, a House of Commons man, John Pym.

And now one final word before we emerge at last from the storm over the gentry. The two scholars whose combined but clashing efforts raised that storm have at least one thing in common. It is the main purpose of both Professor Tawney and Professor Trevor-Roper to show that the 17th century revolution in Britain was due primarily to shifts in the personnel of the landowning classes and shifts in the dimensions of their estates. That a revolution prepared by conflicts over Parliamentary privilege, royal prerogative, judicial independence, arbitrary arrest, power of taxation, and the rule of law in England, triggered by a religious upheaval in Scotland, and traversed by the complex lines of fission that separated Anglican from Puritan, courtier from countryman, is primarily to be explained by the matters that have especially engaged their attention, neither Professor Tawney nor Professor Trevor-Roper has proved. And what such masters of the materials of 17th century history and of historical forensics cannot prove when they set their minds to it, is not likely ever to be proved. Yet the destruction left in the wake of the storm over the gentry need not enduringly depress us. At least one amateur of 17th century history observes the havoc with a sense of relief, even of emancipation. He takes faith and freedom rather seriously himself; and he has not felt that in so doing he is necessarily eccentric. He is inclined to think that a good many men in the mid-17th century took them pretty seriously too. For such a one, it is something of a relief to feel that the outcome of the storm over the gentry licenses him to turn part of his attention from rent rolls, estate accounts, and recognisances of debt to what one very great scholar calls *Liberty and Reformation in the Puritan Revolution.*

Puritanism: A Dynamic Faith

WILLIAM HALLER

William Haller (1885–) was educated at Amherst and Columbia, and taught as Professor of English at the latter university. He is at present a Fellow of the Folger Library, Washington, D. C. He is the author of *Liberty and Reformation in the Puritan Revolution,* referred to by Hexter in the previous excerpt. He has also edited several volumes of Puritan pamphlets, and it is on his profound knowledge of such material that all his generalizations are based.

In Geneva, in Scotland, in Massachusetts, and under peculiar limitations among English sects, Calvinists of one type or another were able to achieve a reformed society in which differences of opinion were checked and uniformity maintained. But throughout England, except under the handicap of persecution, they were permitted to do nothing of the kind. There they had to accommodate themselves year after year as best they could to that peculiar condition which had been set up by the politic Elizabeth and which compelled Englishmen, the more surely the longer it endured, to the maintenance not of religious uniformity but of some sort and degree of toleration as the *sine qua non* of political security and economic prosperity. The reformers, then, unless they were willing to risk ostracism, exile or persecution, had to refrain from too directly assailing the government or their fellow subjects. They were in no position to suppress the people who did not fall in with their ideas, and had to advance their ideas as best they could by the peaceful arts of persuasion. Hence the English Calvinists found that all they could do to advance their cause, though they were for some two generations permitted to do that, was to plead for it by the help of whatever gifts of mind and utterance they happened to possess. Under such conditions they produced, at any rate prior to 1640, no great public leaders, lawgivers and theologians of the stature of Knox and Calvin, but a host of popular propagandists who exploited as never before the potentialities of pulpit and press. Thus Calvinism did not lead to a swift reconstruction of the church but to the creation of a literature which expressed a way of life that eventually far transcended all ecclesiastical and even all religious bounds.

The history of Puritan thought in

From William Haller, *The Rise of Puritanism* (New York, 1938), pp. 84–5, 89–90, 93–4, 95–6, 99–100, 108, 117, 118–19, 123–5, 126–7. Reprinted by permission of the Columbia University Press.

England is primarily the history of the setting forth of the basic doctrine of predestination in terms calculated to appeal to the English populace. The persuasive strength of the doctrine of predestination, as the Puritan preachers presented it, sprang not from its metaphysical but its moral validity. It could, men believed, be proved by inexorable logic out of Scripture, but what really convinced them was its fruitfulness when applied to their own living situation. It was supremely apposite. It supplied a basis both practical and ideal for decision. It suggested an attitude and a line of conduct. Put to the test of experience, it applied and it worked. The concept of universal depravity, by leveling all superiority not of the spirit, enormously enhanced the self-respect of the ordinary man. If none were righteous, then one man was as good as another. God chose whom he would and the distinctions of this world counted for nothing. The concept of free grace still further heightened his confidence. If the only real aristocracy was the aristocracy created by God, then nothing really counted but character and inner worth. Only they were Jews who were Jews inwardly, and the true circumcision was not that of the body. If election were manifested not by outward conformity to an imposed law but by the struggle of the spirit within against the weakness and disobedience of the flesh, then any man might find reason for hope within his own breast. If all this was predestined, then there could be no fear concerning the issue of life's ordeal. "If God be with us, who can be against us?" The triumph of the saints was foreordained. Therefore nothing they could desire was impossible for them to attain. Heaven was theirs already, and if presently they demanded possession of the earth as well, that was no more than human.

The Puritan reformers, balked of their ambition to rule the church but permitted to preach and minister to those they could induce to have them do so, also took to writing books. The fruit of their efforts eventually became a new version of the sacred epic of the fall and regeneration of man. But before we arrive at the epic, we must note how its roots sprang from the personal experience of its creators. Election-vocation-justification-sanctification-glorification was more than an abstract formula. It became the pattern of the most profound experience of men through many generations. From this deep and personal experience grew both the epic and the varied forms in which it was expressed. In the last chapter we traced the worldly activities of the preacher in organizing and extending the work of the spirit in the world. We must now look at the work of the spirit itself within the preachers and within those whom they had persuaded to become one with them in the spirit. This is a task for which they have themselves left us abundant materials. William Perkins in his treatise, *Of the Calling of the Ministerie,* demands how one can "declare the reconciliation betwixt God and Man" who is himself not reconciled. "Dare he present another man to God's mercy for pardon, and never yet presented himself? Can he commend the state of grace to another, and never felt the sweetness thereof in his own soule? Dare he come to preach sanctification with polluted lips, and out of an unsanctified heart? . . . dare any man presume to come into this most high and holy presence of the Lord, untill he have mortified his corruptions, and cast off the unruliness of his affections?" The business of the preacher was to help others along the way into which God had already directed him. The spirit in him, reaching out to the spirit of the sinner still struggling in the darkness, helped it into the light. But first he must himself have been called out of the dark. The conversion he sought to effect he must first have experienced. He could do no less and little more than offer himself as experimental proof of his own teaching. The regenerate testified to the unregenerate, saying, as it were, "I too was a great sinner like Paul and like you, but God having elected me to believe in him, the scales have fallen from my eyes as they may from yours."

"That God pardon'd such a Man in such a Condition is often brought home unto another Man in the same Condition." The most powerful and lasting effect of the popularization of Pauline doctrine to such men as Goodwin was to arouse the most active widespread interest in the inner experience of every individual human being and an almost equally active and widespread activity in giving expression to that interest. Every man was either a convert or susceptible of conversion, and the inner life of any man, once converted, was fraught with daily possibilities for struggle and adventure. It followed that every man's state of spiritual health was the subject of acute concern to the man himself and of sympathetic curiosity to others. Naturally this gave rise to the reporting and comparing of individual case histories, to the endless retailing of confession, reminiscence and anecdote. Out of such, shall we say, spiritual gossip arose a body of legend and a type of popular literature, which was soon to be found quite as edifying and certainly as fascinating as the more formal tracts and sermons. The conditions for the development of such a form of expression were perfect — a generally accepted pattern and opportunities as abundant as life for variations upon a common theme. The devout Puritan turned his back on stage plays and romances, but only in order to look in his own heart and write what happened there. Speaking from the pulpit, the preacher did not as a rule supply explicit personal details, though his teaching was presumed to reflect personal experience. But outside the pulpit, the preacher — and of course common saints were encouraged to follow his example — was free to talk about himself and other people as much as he wished. Not only that, but he very generally kept a journal of his transactions with God and the devil or at least left written record of his conversion. The diary became the Puritan substitute for the confessional, and although few diaries have actually been preserved intact, the substance of many and the fact of their having been kept are apparent in the mass of biographical writing which rapidly accumulated as the Puritan movement progressed.

The test of the saint's conversion was, of course, to be seen in his perseverance in his faith, and faith must be continually active. Each day one sinned, each day one must repent, each day one must be reconciled afresh to God, and each day one must — or at any rate it was advised that one should — enter these circumstances in one's diary. It was of the very essence of Puritan self-discipline that whatsoever thoughts and actions the old Adam within had most desire to keep hidden, the very worst abominations of the heart, one must when one retired to one's private chamber at night draw forth into the light of conscience. To set them down in writing, albeit in some secret "character," was a great help in this. They were the devil incarnate in man and could drag him down to hell. It was also of the essence of Puritan discipline that one should remember and record the good things that happened. These showed the saint that, bad as he was, God had not forsaken him, that God was still taking an intimate and loving interest in his affairs even when bestowing afflictions upon him. Having thus balanced his spiritual books, he could go to bed with a clear conscience, sleep sound and wake with courage. Every evening John Janeway took note

What incomes and profits he received in his spiritual traffique; what returns from that far-country; what answers of prayer, what deadness and flatness, and what observable providences did present themselves, and the substance of what he had been doing; and any wandrings of thoughts, inordinancy in any passions; which, though the world could not discern, he could . . . This made him to retain a grateful remembrance of mercy, and to live in a constant admiring and adoring of divine goodness; this brought him a very intimate acquaintance with his own heart; this kept his spirit low and fitted him for freer communications from God; this made him more lively and active; . . . this made him speak more affectionately and experimentally to others of the things of God: and . . . left a sweet calm upon his spirits, because he every night made even his accounts; and if his sheets should prove his winding-sheet, it had been all one: for, he could say his work was done; so that death could not surprize him.

The pattern to which, under the formula given by Paul in the eighth chapter of Romans, the life of the elect conformed was exemplified by the preachers and set forth in the story of their lives. "I was riding with him into Tunbridge Wells," says Simeon Ashe of Jeremiah Whitaker (d. 1654), "he was pleased to give me the History of his life. . . . Oh how often, and with what meltings, hath he poured forth his heart unto my bosome, in reference to all concernments, personal, relative, private, publick, comfortable and uncomfortable, which have deeply affected him!" Not every feature of the common story appeared full blown in every instance, but the story was characteristically supposed to begin with an account of the horrid sins or scarcely less deplorable dry indifference from which the soul destined to be saved was called and after terrific struggle converted, generally by the reading of some godly book or by the influence of some powerful preacher. Then followed the chronicle, which might be more or less extended according to circumstances, of the saint's lifelong war against the temptation to despair and the other abominations of his heart, lightened only by the encouragements vouchsafed to him by God in the form of good fortune and of worldly and spiritual success. The last scene was the deathbed, one last terrific bout with Satan and then triumph and glory forever after. Along with the sermons and treatises in which they anatomized the spiritual life and with the diaries and confessional biographies in which they and their proselytes depicted the workings of God in particular cases, the preachers also took to setting forth the pattern of daily existence which the saint should follow. Let us glance for a moment at the ideal day of the elect, as described in *A Garden of Spirituall Flowers*[1] and the many other popular presentations of the Puritan code. The saint is told to awake with God and pray. "And let this bee done solemnely upon thy knees (and not as many doe, lazing upon their beds) that it may bee done with a humble, pure, and sincere devotion." If he is the head of a household, he should be stirring early to call his family together for morning prayers. After breakfast he may betake himself to his ordinary calling and business, seeing that his family does likewise. There are "Rules for the behaving of himself Christian-like in imployment about his worldly businesse, and enjoying the benefit of the same." He must keep close watch upon his heart, words and deeds, and see that his time is not idly, carelessly or unprofitably spent. He must mind his own business and let other men mind theirs. "Be not a Tale-bearer, nor a Tale-receiver: deale justly and uprightly with all men: let thy conversation be without covetousnesse, and without prodigalitie: serve the Lord in singlenesse of heart: be doing good, and abstaine from all appearance of evill." In the same spirit he is told how to bear himself in company and in solitude, in prosperity and in adversity. He is not to shun prosperity nor yet to set his heart upon it. If it comes, it will come as God's free gift and is to be used as such. He is not to fear the adversity which God may bestow for the strengthening of his spirit. Business done, he goes home and concludes the day by gathering his household once more about him. He reads to them from scripture, catechizes them, sings psalms and prays with them. Then he goes to his chamber to meditate and, as we have seen, to balance his spiritual accounts. And so to bed. For Sundays, he is given special

[1] The book is by Richard Rogers, preacher at Wethersfield, Essex, in the late 16th and early 17th centuries. [Editor's note]

directions. In church, whither he proceeds in the morning at the head of his family, he must keep his eyes fixed on the preacher, so that thoughts may not wander. He is advised to mark the speaker's text, observe how it is "divided," note the handling of each division, find the places in scripture alleged for proof, fold down the leaf at the appropriate passages so that he may review them at leisure. Then home again to discuss the sermon with the family after dinner and back again to church to repeat the whole performance in the afternoon. If such a program seem preposterous to the man of the present day, he should remember that his forefathers even in the conduct of this world's business were concerned about their consciences. Perhaps the desire of later generations to escape from Puritanism has been at least in part a desire to do business with less hindrance from a scheme of life so insistent upon keeping the individual forever in mind of his moral responsibilities.

The Puritan code was much more than a table of prohibitions. It was the program of an active, not a monastic or contemplative, life. The saints stripped themselves for battle, and only as the battle waxed hot and desperate did they degenerate into the fanatical iconoclasts of familiar tradition. Milton's lady scorned not the gifts that Comus offered her but the giver. "Worldly things," according to Sibbes, "are good in themselves, and given to sweeten our passage to Heaven," and to sweeten our "profession of Religion." We must use the world as our servant, not our master, take comfort in it but not set our hearts upon it, or let ourselves be made "drunke with the cares below." All is, in other words, as we have grace to use it. "This world and the things thereof are all good, and were all made of God, for the benefit of his creature." John Dod, gathering his flock about him, opening his door to all comers, sitting down at the head of a full table, talking himself thirsty, and calling for a draft of wine and beer mixed, was no bigoted ascetic, though he did disapprove of stage plays, dancing and card-playing. The saint

had no reason to fear the world or run away from it. Rather he must go forth into it and do the will of God there. Rogers scorns the suggestion that, if men live according to the godly rule, they will neglect their necessary affairs "and so poverty grow upon the land." On the contrary, he says, he who goes about his work, not attending upon God by faith, "goeth about it preposterously, and shal find his successe answerable." "He riddeth not most worke, who goeth to it most early, when his instruments which he should use in the performance of the same be blunt and dull." "Godliness hinders not men's labours, neither decaies the Common-wealth." There is "godly thrift," a "Christian gaining," and a "lawfull prospering" which come to him who goes to work "with a mind which is at peace with God." Who cannot see that by the labor of such men "the Common-wealth. . . should flourish much more, having a certeine promise of blessing?"

The saint knows that he need not fear to lose a penny while he stops to say his prayers. He knows that whatever he has and whatever he gains in the course of business comes from God. His prime piece of capital, he knows, consists in the abilities and opportunities which God has bestowed upon him for doing the business of the world. They are his talent, and he never forgets by whom this was given and on what terms it will be exacted in return. This doctrine comes, of course, directly from the parable of the talents, "wherein," to use the words of Gabriel Powell, "is shewed, that no man, of what state or condition hee bee, is Lord of his owne riches or substance, but the steward and disposer of it, accountable unto God for all things." It is the theme of Milton's sonnet concerning the one talent which is death to hide. Our individual abilities are not given us as rewards to be enjoyed — no sinner merits any favor from God. Nor does God grant them as necessary means to ends of his own — "God doth not need either men's work or his own gifts." They are bestowed as unconditional occasions for service upon such as truly love their maker. Those who put their gifts to work, or, as Milton would have it, merely stand ready and waiting to do so, may feel assured that they please him. Those who do not may expect one day to hear the master chide. For, to quote Powell once more, "we must be accountable for the least farthing which we have received of God; after what manner we came by it, how and to what use we have bestowed and spent it."

No part of the Puritan code was more weighted with practical significance than this. Nothing in the postulates of Puritan doctrine up to this point was inconsistent with the stopping of Puritanism at mere pietism within self-centred groups of believers, and such pietistic groups did in fact spring up within the Puritan movement as among Protestants on the continent. But by insistence upon the moral aspects of the doctrine of the talent the preachers opened a wide door through which they drove their flocks out into the world to have their fill of experience. To be specific, they gave in this way to the general doctrine of God's calling a definite application. When God called his elect to repent and believe, he also called upon them to act. The gifts and opportunities, no matter how humble and narrow, with which the saint was invested were also part of his commission from God. Whatsoever we undertake in the exercise of our talents and in the spirit of faith is good. It is what God has called us to do.

What was true for men in other occupations was no less but no more true for the preacher, though his task was harder. He should, said Rogers, follow the rule laid down for every believer, and then he must also follow his special calling, which was to preach. He must have the gift for admonishing, exhorting, comforting and instructing others. He must demonstrate his possession of the gift by securing acknowledgment of its presence in him from those he would serve. He must be able to inspire his hearers to put their own talents to use. His lot was, indeed, not an easy one. Preachers must have more capacious souls than ordinary men since their work was both more difficult and more important, but they had therefore greater trials and temptations to endure. "Though it must be granted, that they have many more helps in regard to their ministry than private men; yet . . . their troubles and crosses are manie more and greater . . . for they are more shot at by Satan and his instruments, they have many discouragements, unkindnesses offered them, and hatred for their good will and for doing of their duty."

Such assertions of the special duty and the special danger of preaching in the exercise of their special gift are almost as numerous in the preachers' sermons as the sermons themselves. According to the doctrine of the talent, the only responsibility that could possibly equal theirs was that of the magistrate. These two, in fact, the vocation of the one to preach and of the other to rule, were the poles about which the truly godly state revolved. This principle was presently to be the basic contention of Milton when he took up the argument for Utopia. John Downame presented it much earlier and with admirable clearness. "Princes and Magistrates," he says, perform their services to God, "by enacting good lawes, and seeing them duely executed, making their owne lives (as it were) rules of that obedience which they require of the people, and lively examples and patternes for their imitation." Preachers serve "by leading those which are committed unto their charge, in the waies of truth and godlinesse, not onely by their preaching and writing, instruction, admonition, perswasion and exhortation, but also by practizing those duties which they teach others, and shining before them in the light of a godly life." It will follow, if each has exercised his talent in the fear of the Lord, that the people will also strive to please God, "by yeelding their cheerefull obedience to the godly lawes of Governors, and by imbracing the sound and profitable doctrine, and imitating the christian and religious examples of their godly Teachers." Thus did the preachers link the doctrine of the talent with their conception of the dual state, one part carnal, the other spiritual, the two complementary. They were, perhaps, dreaming of such a theocracy as indeed they achieved for a time in New England, but they were also, certainly without intention, preparing for a society in which popular education and the free play of public opinion must become the conditions under which and by which government must operate.

Eminent Puritan Laymen Form an Interest Group

J. H. HEXTER

WE may first ask ourselves in what kinds of enterprise we may find the Puritans acting together, or, better, in what activities they collaborated *as Puritans*. After the death of Archbishop Bancroft in 1610, primacy in the English Church fell to George Abbott. As long as Abbott controlled the machinery of ecclesiastical discipline, the Puritans found room enough in the Church for their way of worship. The Archbishop did not seek to check them; probably in all questions except that of episcopal government his heart was with them. More than a decade of salutary neglect gave the Puritans a sense of security from which they but slowly aroused themselves when the hour of disaster overtook them. Gradually the influence of the Primate waned; gradually William Laud and his friends found favor at court for their catholicizing ideals.[1]

When Laud, first as Bishop of London and then as Abbott's successor at Canterbury, set his hand to extirpating the Puritan element (he might have said the "Puritan excrescences") in the Church, men to whom that element was the food of life and the light of salvation had to bestir themselves. Laud's policy left two ways open to them: they could fight or they could flee; but they could only fight as the conquered fight, secretly and by craft. For the King had disarmed them, had taken from them their only effective weapon of open resistance, by ruling without Parliament for eleven years.

So the Puritans planned for flight, for a mass exodus, in a series of colonizing schemes. Of these schemes the projected Puritan refuge on the little Isle of Providence in the West Indies makes the best starting place for our investigation. The project is closely associated with the Civil War Parliament. Indeed, one contemporary[2] will have us believe it was the very seed from which that Parliament grew. This earliest and most naïve exponent of the *complot* conception of the Puritan uprising tells us that the whole affair was concocted in the rooms of Providence Island Company in Gray's Inn Lane. Without subscribing to this neat and simple theory of revolution, we may admit that an uncommonly large number of men later prominent on the Roundhead side wasted time and money on the Providence Island scheme. The company for the plantation

[1] Hexter explains in a note that the ideals were Anglo-Catholic, not Roman Catholic. ([Editor's note]

[2] The pamphleteer "Mercurius Civicus." [Editor's note]

Reprinted by permission of the publishers from Jack H Hexter, *The Reign of King Pym* (Cambridge, Mass., Harvard University Press, 1941), pp. 76–84.

of the Island of Providence was chartered in 1630. Heading the list of adventurers are three of the greatest Puritan peers — William, Viscount Say and Sele, whose bailiwick of Banbury was said to be the most Puritan town in England; Robert, Baron Brook, confirmed in Puritanism by his education in Calvinist Holland; and Robert, Earl of Warwick, who used a private fleet he inherited from his father in profitable anti-Spanish piracy of a more or less high-minded Puritan kind. No less important in Roundhead affairs than the three lords were three commoners among the Providence Island adventurers — Sir Thomas Barrington, intimate of Warwick and his deputy lieutenant in Essex, head of the Puritan Barrington family, and related one way or another to most of the big Puritan families in the eastern counties; Oliver St. John, counsel for John Hampden in the ship-money case, and in 1640 one of the authors of the petition of the twelve peers for calling a Parliament; and, finally, St. John's collaborator on the peers' petition, John Pym himself. Excepting two London merchants, who dropped out early in the history of the Providence Island Company, there were altogether twenty-six adventurers. Of the twenty-six almost two-thirds sat in the upper or lower house of the Long Parliament, and there was not a single Royalist in the lot.

Saybrook, an earlier projected Puritan colony, was not a costly failure, but it was not a ravishing success either. It took its name from two of the grandees of the Providence Island Company. Other participants in the West Indian venture had joined Lords Say and Brook in planning a settlement on the Connecticut shore of Long Island Sound: Sir Nathaniel Rich, Henry Darley, and again the Earl of Warwick and John Pym. Besides these in the list of patentees for Saybrook we find three other names that were to loom large in the era of the Puritan Revolution: Henry Lawrence, elected to the Civil War Parliament in 1646, and later president of Cromwell's Council of State; Arthur Haselrig,

the regicide republican, executed at the Restoration for his part in the trial of Charles I; and the patriot John Hampden, the champion of English liberty every schoolboy knows.

The Providence Island and Saybrook ventures were anything but brilliant triumphs of colonizing activity. One Puritan attempt at colonization succeeded beyond the fondest dream of the most sanguine of its backers. Several patentees of Saybrook and adventurers for the Providence Plantation had earlier subscribed to the stock of the Massachusetts Bay Company, the pathetic little enterprise that grew into the greatest of all the colonies of England. Also in the list of the original subscribers we find the names of almost a dozen members of the Long Parliament, among them John White, family lawyer to the Winthrops and legal guide to the Bay Company. Again all these members were Roundheads in the Civil War.

The overlapping lists of adventurers, patentees, and subscribers interested in colonizing schemes in the New World tell us part of the story of a close-knit Puritan connection before the Civil War, but they do not tell the whole story. For another chapter we may turn to the correspondence of John Winthrop, to whom more than to any other man the Massachusetts Bay Company owed its success. Winthrop maintained contact between the Bay Company and the Saybrook patentees by regular correspondence with George Fenwick, the American agent for the the Connecticut venture; but the connection between the Lincolnshire[3] squire and the Puritan magnates antedates the founding of the New England colonies, and in part followed channels independent of the immediate business problems of the New World settlements. Sir Nathaniel Rich, Sir Arthur Haselrig, Henry Darley, and Herbert Pelham, all Saybrook patentees, appear as old friends in Winthrop's letters. Darley and Pelham had both been to New England,

[3] This should read "Suffolk." [Editor's note]

the latter serving as first treasurer to Harvard College. Another old New Englander and old friend to the Winthrops was John Gurdon of the Providence Island Adventureres. The lords who gave their name to Saybrook also knew Winthrop well; and although some coldness grew between them, in 1637 the Massachusetts governor received a brotherly letter from his "loving friend, R. Brooke."

English Puritans not active in colonial affairs were still deeply interested in the fate of the experiment in New England. They rejoiced in its triumphs, and mourned its misfortunes, and felt it to be, in a way, a thing of their own. They exchange letters with Winthrop or appear in his correspondence as old associates and friends. Among them is the Puritan peer, the Earl of Lincoln. Sir Henry Vane the younger crops up in Winthrop's letter, as he did in Winthrop's life and in the early life of the Bay Colony, a disturbing, enigmatic force. Three Puritans who followed curiously divergent paths in the Civil War Parliament find a common starting place in the Winthrop correspondence. Alexander Rigby, a hard-bitten Commonwealthman, distinguished by his early claim of the right to tax for the two Houses, appears in the Winthrop papers, tangled with Sir Ferdinando Gorges in a fight over the Maine patent. Our old friend Sir Simond Dewes, the peace-loving diarist, knew Winthrop in the days before the exodus to Massachusetts. And Sir John Clotworthy, a fiery spirit to Dewes, to republican Rigby a dangerous Royalist, wrote to Winthrop in the days of Laud of the worship of God now "pompous in the outward but penurious in the inward part." But of all the letters Winthrop received, the one from Henry Lawrence — Saybrook patentee, member of the Civil War Parliament, president of the Protectorate Council of State — best shows how profoundly the hope of a New World refuge moved the English Puritans. "My faith makes me willing to outrun my intelligence in congratulating your safe arrival in New England.

For God hath already showed Himself so gracious in conducting those who have gone your way, as we may . . . venture to trust without any further trial."

We have said that the Puritans had to flee from the Laudian regime or fight it, but that after 1629 they could make no frontal attack on the new ecclesiastical order because they had lost their only offensive weapon, Parliament. They waged a losing guerilla war against Laud, but we cannot pause to follow the history of that war. To do so would take us into every parish in England where a Puritan had the right of presentation, to every parish where the local gentry showed their dislike of the new practices of the new priesthood, to every parish where a Puritan mob tore down an altar screen or heaved rocks at an idolatrous picture-glass window. We can only glance in passing at one of the curious episodes in this resistance, the work of the feoffees of impropriations and its adjunct the "seminary" of St. Anthony's[4] in London. After going through one of the properly Puritan colleges at Oxford or Cambridge, promising young preachers would get practical training in a lectureship at Puritan-controlled St. Anthony's. In the meantime a group of zealous men gathered contributions to buy up lay impropriations, that is, the ecclesiastical income of tithes that had fallen into the hands of laymen, especially at the time of the Reformation. To the disgust of the Laudian faction, the feoffees did not use the purchased tithes to restore full livings to the ministers in the impropriated parishes. Instead they employed the income from the tithes to establish lectureships and buy benefices for "godly ministers," that is, for bright young Puritans. Before the feoffees had got very far in their work, Laud took alarm and suppressed them. Before the suppression there had been seventeen feoffees. Seven of the seventeen were interested in colonizing schemes, including Christopher Sherland of the Providence Island Company and

---

[4] At this period, usually written "St. Antholin's." [Editor's note]

John White, whom we met just a while back.

Richard Baxter remarks somewhere that the opposition to Charles I ran in two separate streams, religious and political, and that in the Long Parliament the King had to face two sorts of enemies — church enemies and state enemies. Such a distinction, on the face of it, seems dubious; if there are fifteen possible reasons for disliking a man, we most probably will dislike him not for one reason but for all fifteen. To confirm our doubt of Baxter's classification we need not rely on the *cause célèbre* against the King's arbitrary power, the case of ship money, when opposition to taxation without consent found its leaders in two great Puritans — Lord Say and Sele and John Hampden. We need not even point out how happily (or how unpleasantly) black-letter legalism blended with blue-Sunday Puritanism in a William Prynne. We may look back beyond the later Puritan attacks on prerogative government and examine briefly the first attempt to resist the arbitrary policy of Charles I. The matter at issue had nothing to do with purity of religious doctrine or simplicity of religious worship; it had to do with the forced loan of 1627. Resisting ecclesiastical innovation was a complicated and touchy business. Resisting a forced loan was the easiest thing in the world; one merely refused to pay — and went to prison.

A glance down the list of resisters for names of Long Parliament men brings us up with a start. The first name that strikes us is that of Thomas Wentworth. For a few days he sat in the upper house of the Long Parliament. Then as Earl of Strafford, councillor to Charles I in all evil things, he died on the block, attainted of treason, forsaken by the King he served so well. Yet Wentworth's refusal to pay need not make us despair of establishing the essentially Puritan character of the resistance to the forced loan. He was but one of twenty

Long Parliament men among the resisters. Without exception the other nineteen were Roundheads, from the moderate Sir Harbottle Grimston to the regicide Sir John Danvers. Future members of all three Puritan colonizing companies are represented among the men who refused to lend in 1627: Samuel Vassal of the Massachusetts Bay Company, Sir Thomas Barrington and Sir Gilbert Gerard of the Providence Island Adventurers, and Richard Knightly and John Hampden of the Saybrook patentees. There are other distinguished Puritan names on the list: Sir William Masham, Sir Harbottle Grimston, Sir Nathaniel Barnardiston, all future elders of the Presbyterian Church established by the Civil War Parliament. Barnardiston was an old friend of John Winthrop. So was Sir Francis Barrington, head of the Puritan Barrington family in 1627. While Barrington was in jail for refusing the loan, the elder Winthrop sent young John to him with remembrances of love. Thus in the vanguard of the first attack on the King's secular policy we find the Puritans. And this is only natural. The state policy of Charles I and his church policy are too much of a piece to box off into separate compartments. Opposition to the latter almost inevitably entailed opposition to the former.

We have traced the activities of the Puritans before the Civil War in colonization and in resistance to Charles's churchmanship and statesmanship. We have seen that many leaders of Puritan colonization and resistance sat in the Long Parliament. We have seen, too, that the Puritan enterprises were not each the work of a different group. A number of the leaders had their fingers in several Puritan pies. The analogy that immediately suggests itself to us is ultramodern. The active Puritan groups remind us of nothing so much as a *congeries* of independent corporations with directorates conveniently interlocking. . . .

The Decline of the Council and the Loss of Royal Control over Parliament

DAVID H. WILLSON

Born in 1901, and educated at Haverford and Cornell, Willson is now Professor of History at the University of Minnesota. He has been associated with Notestein and others in work on parliamentary diaries of the early seventeenth century. His most recent work is a biography of James I. The comparisons which Willson makes show yet again that, in order to understand the early seventeenth century, we need to know what happened in the reign of Elizabeth I, how institutions worked in that earlier period, and what men thought about them.

THE Tudor genius for government, which remains the admiration of posterity, evolved a form of absolutism that was not incompatible with the growth of the house of commons. That growth was, in fact, astonishingly rapid under the Tudors. When Henry VII secured the throne, the commons were still in the medieval stage of their development, with little organization or influence. When Elizabeth died in 1603, they had secured an established place in the counsels of the nation, their house was on an equality with that of the lords, their privileges were becoming realities, and they were ready, though they would have been the first to deny it, to make a successful bid for sovereignty in the decades ahead. But if Henry VIII and Elizabeth tolerated and at times encouraged this development, it was because they were able to direct and control it to a large extent. They did this chiefly through the force of their own dominant personalities and through their skill and adroitness in dealing with the commons. But they relied also upon their councillors and other officials who were members of the house. The sovereign remained in the background and left the details of parliamentary management to the more invisible guidance of his ministers. These men, clustered in a group close to the speaker, formed a sort of ministerial bench and were, in fact, the leaders of the house. They initiated the most important legislation, they made clear the need for subsidies, and under Elizabeth they formed a breakwater against the increasing demands of the commons for more liberty in the house and for less autocratic methods of government in church and state.

As the end of the reign approached, opposition became more open and the commons more difficult to control. Councillors were treated with disrespect. Disorderly scenes took place in the commons during the parliament of 1601. Members protested when they were told that there were topics they must not discuss. "When any great or weighty matter or Bill is here handled," the council was told, "we streight say it toucheth the Prerogative and must not be medled withal." Committees were growing larger in membership and thus more difficult to handle; they also dealt with larger topics than the details of single measures. Once the great figure of the queen was removed and the commons found themselves in the altered atmosphere of a new dynasty to

From *The Privy Councillors in the House of Commons, 1603–1629*, by David Harris Willson, University of Minnesota Press, pp. 3, 12–23. Copyright 1940 by the University of Minnesota.

which they were not bound by long-established ties of affection and loyalty, opposition might well flare up with unexpected violence.

Precisely at the moment when the crown faced dangerous opposition in parliament and was forced to do battle for its place in the constitution, its position was undermined by the weaknesses and errors of the new ruler and by the rapid decline of the council as an instrument of government.

James, as everybody knows, was quite unfit to guide the commons at a most delicate moment in their history; and his personal relations with parliament were disastrous. He was not the fool that the scandalmongers at court would have us believe. He was not without flashes of political insight and a sense of reality. "He needs no spectacles," wrote the Venetian ambassador, "and when he wishes to see he is like an Argus." His faults were less those of unintelligence than of bad training and of basic weakness of character.

His struggle with the Presbyterian clergy in Scotland inculcated in him an exaggerated dislike of puritanism; and blinded him to the distinction between radical forms of dissent and the moderate puritan tendencies of many members of the house of commons. All puritans were suspect because their conceptions of church government undermined the power of the bishops and hence the power of the king. There was thus no place for a large comprehension in the English church. James, of very necessity, had parried the claims of the Scottish divines by a corresponding exaltation, in theory at least, of the position of the crown. Monarchy became the supremest thing on earth, kings little gods, and "the laws were but craved by his subjects and only made by him." Such theories fitted nicely with James's high opinion of himself. But they rendered unnecessary and ridiculous the caution and restraint of Elizabeth in dealing with the commons. To James the veto was a prerogative to be employed at will; the privileges of the commons mere examples of royal indulgence; and the demand

for change mere clamor. Thus he presented a blind conservatism to the aspirations of the commons; all novelties are dangerous, he told them; and his answer was purely negative at all points. In these conceptions the adroit Tudor combination of outward toleration and quiet conciliar control could find no place.

In Scotland James had governed by canny manipulation of rival factions, by sowing dissensions among his adversaries, by combining intrigue and sharp practices with a show of force. In England these methods produced chaos and stalemate at court and mere meddling in dealings with the commons.

James took a deep interest in parliament, following day by day or even hour by hour the fortunes of measures he desired. He demanded from his ministers long reports of parliamentary business. He interfered far too much, often without just cause, in the work of the commons, emphasizing the intrusion of the crown where Elizabeth had sought to minimize it. His meddling raised minor disputes to the dignity of constitutional issues and provoked heated rejoinders. He cheapened his speeches by their frequency, their scolding and didactic tone, and their references to the divine right of kings. His bearing was awkward and undignified, in striking contrast to that of the stately Elizabeth. "When he wishes to speak like a king," wrote Tillières, the French ambassador, "he rails like a tyrant and when he wishes to yield he does so with indecency." He could be astonishingly tactless. He told the commons, as an argument in favor of union with Scotland, that England had often been conquered in the past but Scotland never. As the Venetian ambassador remarked, James had a wonderful faculty for doing himself harm.

He was a very lazy person. He loved to make a speech or preside over a disputation, and did both quite well. But the daily routine of attention to business, no small part of Tudor success, was abhorrent to him, and he lacked the power of will to follow it through. In 1605 he seriously proposed to the council that all business be placed in their hands and that he be left free to enjoy a quiet country life. For a time after Salisbury's death he attempted to be his own secretary and "took delight to show his readiness and ability in those causes"; but very soon "that vigour began to relent and he must daily more and more attend to his own health and quiet." The Venetian ambassador wrote in 1620 that James "seemed utterly weary of the affairs that were taking place all over the world at this time, and hated being obliged every day to spend time over unpleasant matters and listen to nothing but requests and incitements to move in every direction and to meddle with everything. He remarked: I am not God Almighty. His dependence upon favorites was in part the result of indolence; it was so easy to settle affairs by doing as the favorite wished. But government in England still required the close and constant scrutiny of the sovereign. Without it, honesty and efficiency quickly declined and money went like water. A session of parliament, moreover, greatly increased the need for attention to affairs.

The demands of business combined with minor physical ailments to aggravate James's natural petulance and irritability. He easily flew into petty fits of rage that could do great harm. The commons were extremely irritating; but caution, temper, and self-restraint were absolutely essential if the king was to deal with them successfully. Three of James's four parliaments were dissolved by the king in fits of anger. Whitehall was a hectic place at best, and James made matters worse by relaxing the rules governing access to the sovereign. He found himself confused by the diversity of counsel and harassed by the importunity of suitors. Calvert wrote in 1610 that the king was "so distracted with variety of Opinions, from a Number about him, especially Scots, that though he would, he cannot resolve that which he desires; which is the Cause that so often as he can he absents himself from the Town, yet is quickly fetched again on every Occasion,

which much troubles him." He spent long periods in the country not only because he hated London and loved hunting but because he sought escape from the irritations and worries of the court. The Venetian ambassador wrote in 1621 that James gladly went on progress to free himself from the annoyance of ministers and ambassadors and to get as far away from them as possible.

But such absences interfered with business. "The Lords of the Council," wrote the Venetian ambassador in 1607, "have with great justice pointed out to his Majesty that his continued absence from the city, especially while the question of the Union is on, is very injurious to the negotiations." Two of the most serious parliamentary crises of the reign found James loitering in the country. "It is much marvelled," wrote Chamberlain in 1621, "that so much business being now afoot, both at home and abroad, the king should keep still at Newmarket."

As James grew older his weaknesses grew upon him; and he became irresolute and timid. "It seems to me that the intelligence of this king has diminished," wrote Tillières in 1621; "not that he cannot act firmly and well at times and particularly when the peace of the kingdom is involved, but such efforts are not so continual as they once were. His mind uses its powers only for a short time, but in the long run he is cowardly." His timidity, wrote Tillières again, "has increased day by day as old age carries him into apprehensions and vices diminish his intelligence." "The king seems very anxious and perplexed," wrote the Venetian ambassador; "as a matter of fact his Majesty is vexed by great irresolution and does not know what to do." These tendencies reached their climax during the journey of Charles and Buckingham to Madrid. To James this was a period of mental agony, in which he "spent some nights in unbroken fury," a prey to the darkest fears and apprehensions. It left him an old man too weak in will to resist his son and his favorite. When they urged him to call parliament in 1624, he could resist only by sinking into a state of distracted inaction, "sometimes swearing and calling upon God, heaven, and the angels, at other times weeping, then laughing, and finally pretending illness in order to play upon the pity of those who urge him to generous actions and to show them that sickness renders him incapable of deciding anything, demanding only repose and, indeed, the tomb." These things are well known; yet they cannot be forgotten in a study of the house of commons.

As the quality of the ruler declined, so did that of his council. This was not noticeable, however, during the first ten years of the reign. James inherited from Elizabeth her chief minister, Robert Cecil, now earl of Salisbury, who made himself the pivot about which the entire machinery of government revolved and whose position resembled that of a modern prime minister, responsible for administration and legislation alike. But if he, more than a president, was alpha and omega in council, he nevertheless, as he said, did not like to carry great things alone. He constantly consulted his colleagues and was merely the first among the councillors of the king. The council was active during these years, and James left affairs very largely in its hands. Foreign observers came to the conclusion that it was the council that ruled the country. "The Council spares the King the trouble of governing," wrote the Venetian ambassador, "and not only do all subjects transact their business with it, but foreign representatives as well, and one might say it was the very ears, body, and voice of the King." Again he wrote that James "remits everything to the Council," and "has virtually given it full and absolute authority." Such statements, while overcharged, indicate the high place that the council, dominated by Salisbury, occupied at this time. As long as he lived it retained its Tudor characteristics.

After his death in 1612 the council entered upon a rapid decline. Of many causes, two are pre-eminent: the factional strife of contending groups and the rise of government through favorites to the neglect of the council as a whole. Once Salisbury was removed, new opinions and influences, which he had suppressed or excluded, quickly emerged, and we enter upon a new phase of the reign. The Howards, with their Spanish and pro-Catholic sympathies, were already entrenched in the favor of the king before Salisbury's death, and now their influence was greatly increased. The mainspring of the Spanish faction was Henry Howard, earl of Northampton. He was supported by the other Howards, Suffolk, who became lord treasurer, and Nottingham, the lord admiral. The Howards placed many of their dependents, such as Sir Thomas Lake and Sir Charles Cornwallis, in places of trust; and eventually they joined forces with the favorite, Robert Carr, who became earl of Somerset. They formed but a fraction of the council, but they held many of the most important offices, had the aid of Sarmiento (later Count Gondomar) who came to England in 1613, and could rely upon James's obsession for a Spanish marriage alliance. The Howards were a worthless and treacherous lot, ready to sacrifice the interests of the nation for their own ends. An anti-Spanish group of ministers was led by Ellesmere, the lord chancellor, Abbot, the austere archbishop of Canterbury, Pembroke, "always the mortal enemy of Spain," Southampton, whose impetuosity did as much harm as good, and the ultra-Protestant secretaries, Winwood and Naunton. Faction in the council was, of course, nothing new. But the Spanish and anti-Spanish groups opposed each other on fundamentals: on parliament, religion and foreign policy. Their animosities had a deep and disastrous effect upon the relations of king and commons.

The Spanish party was momentarily weakened in 1618, when the Howards fell from power, Gondomar returned to Spain, and the Thirty Years' War began in Germany. The war caused Protestant and anti-Spanish sentiment to flare up at court and in the council. Abbot, Southampton, Pembroke, and Naunton urged James to intervene; other councillors — Mandeville, Bacon, Hamilton, Coke, Edmondes — were ready for a strong anti-Spanish policy; and Buckingham, now the arbiter of patronage, joined the war party. Gondomar wrote that everything was spoiled in England since his departure, and James complained almost in tears that he was surrounded by three hundred Winwoods. But with Gondomar's return in March, 1620, and Buckingham's defection from the war party in the following summer, former divisions reappeared in the council. Buckingham carried a number of other councillors with him; Gondomar regained his old ascendancy over the king; and the Spanish faction seemed stronger than ever. It remained in the ascendant until Charles and Buckingham returned from Madrid in 1623 with a new policy and a determination to crush pro-Spanish sentiment in their ministers.

It was the tragedy of James that he turned for advice to favorites and ministers connected with the Spanish faction and neglected the council as a whole. As early as 1612 the Spanish ambassador noted that James "maketh little or noe account at all of his Councillors and scarcely communicateth with them anything of importance." In 1613 Gondomar wrote of the sudden importance attained by Carr, then Viscount Rochester: "The Viscount Rochester at the Council Table showeth much temper and modesty, without seeming to press and sway anything. But afterward the King resolveth all business with him alone, both those that pass by Council, and many others, wherewith he never maketh them acquainted." Commissioners were appointed in 1617 to deal with the Spanish match, and thus remove it from the hands of the council. This exclusion of councillors from important affairs tended to increase. By 1620 Buckingham had risen from an amanuensis and boon companion of the king to a counsellor of the greatest importance. During his early years at court he had cared little about affairs of state, and Gondomar had written in 1615 that "nothing of importance had appeared as yet to pass through

his hands." But now he advised the king to the exclusion of older and more experienced men. Gondomar's influence was even more astonishing. "His proceedings pass with great secrecy," wrote the Venetian ambassador in 1620, "for the most part alone with the king, as he once intimated that he hated even the presence of the Secretaries of State, so they are politely requested to leave the room. Many of the leading Lords of the Council doubt whether his Majesty communicates to them all the things he treats of with the said ambassador." "He is not only an ambassador," wrote Tillières who, it must be confessed, was consumed with jealousy, "but one of the first councillors of state of this kingdom, being day and night at the palace of Whitehall, where the most secret counsels are not only communicated to him, but where they listen to his own advises and follow them almost to the letter." "Some of the ministers here call him a new councillor to his Majesty."

Thus private advisers took the place of government by council. The Venetian ambassador wrote in 1622, "The old ministers and those who look upon matters otherwise than the king desires, know little or nothing of the king's proceedings, as he avoids all except two or three strong partisans of Spain." The actual direction of affairs was in the hands of the king, the favorite, the prince, "and four or five of the cabinet, all well disposed to Spain." When Charles was in Madrid, negotiating the Spanish match, he wrote his father, "I beseech your Majestie advyse as littel with your Counsell in these businesses as you can"; and James replied, "Ye neede not doubte but I will be warrie enough in not acquainting my counsell with any secreate in youre letres." When Charles and Buckingham came to power, the council was neglected more than ever. By 1626 the Venetian ambassador wrote that "there is no longer any council, as Buckingham alone with three or four of his creatures for show constitute it." "They have introduced a privy council," said Wentworth in the commons. A leading minister told the Venetian ambassador in 1626 that no council meeting had been summoned for a long time in any matter of importance.

The council was abused as well as neglected. Councillors who differed from the king were browbeaten into silence, and divergence of opinion was regarded as factiousness or stupidity. When certain councillors defended Raleigh in 1618, James declared heatedly that he would do as he saw fit "without following the advice of fools and badly disposed persons." Opposition to the dissolution of parliament in 1621 was treated with insolence and bullied into silence. James told the council that the pope approved the Spanish match, not to impart information, but "to render everyone dumb." In 1623 councillors were forced to pledge their support to the Spanish marriage treaty and then to denounce it. Treatment of this kind, along with constant fear of dismissal, crushed all independence of judgment. When in 1628, in a meeting of the council, Buckingham suddenly asked the king to summon parliament, it was thought a piece of acting to induce other councillors to express their opinions. But no one said a word. The council had learned only too well its lesson of silent obedience. It was also abused in other ways. It was told of plans and policies merely to share the opprobrium with which those plans and policies were regarded by the public. Its opinion was sought to give a semblance of sobriety to fantastic schemes. Its authority was abused in collecting the forced loan of 1627.

Thus "the king used his council merely for show"; and it became "a mere shadow for ordinary affairs, to toil about providing money and to edit matters which are intended for publication." The council, excluded from a share in shaping national policy, devoted itself to administrative routine: the supervision and repair of public works, forts, and bridges; musters and military matters; Ireland, the Channel Islands, and the colonies; innumerable details of local government; much judicial work; and the regulation of commerce and industry. But all these things belonged to the details of government.

This development was emphasized by the increasing number of members who were essentially bureaucrats rather than statesmen. Councillors such as Sir George Calvert, Sir Robert Naunton, Sir Thomas Lake, Sir Lionel Cranfield, Sir Richard Weston, Sir John Coke, and later Sir Francis Windebank, many of whom rose to power with Buckingham, owed their places primarily to their industry and efficiency in detailed administration. To place administration in their hands was in many ways fortunate. They raised the standard of official honesty and saw to it that the crown was not cheated by every tradesman with whom it did business. But with the exception of Cranfield, none of these men had the making of statesmen. They were capable clerks who could take care of wearisome details and carry out instructions. They were content with routine matters and made no pretense to statesmanship on any higher plane. They paid abject homage to the favorite; and their letters breathe an atmosphere of submissive acceptance of their subordinate role. In a word, the king and Buckingham were not looking for advisers in the council, but for men who would do as they were told. And this was what they were getting. Personal government was replacing statesmen with bureaucrats, men who could work efficiently but without initiative or imagination. It was from their number that the councillors who served in the commons were largely drawn.

Other causes contributed to the council's decline. Many appointments to the council were open to question and aimed at other things than building an able body of advisers. James regarded membership somewhat as a mark of royal favor, as if it were another rank in the nobility; and Charles and Buckingham filled the council with their creatures. Many councillors, wrote the Venetian ambassador, were frivolous courtiers, better fitted to manipulate goblets than to deal with affairs. In an attempt to balance factions, James appointed men of radically different points of view. Thus Winwood, the ultra-Protestant, balanced Lake, the Catholic; and Naunton balanced Calvert in the same way. Gardiner has analyzed the council's membership about 1617 and finds it very heterogeneous. The churchmen represented different schools of theology; the secretaries supported different policies; some councillors urged a French and some a Spanish marriage for the prince. Another ruler might have found such a council an admirable basis upon which to form an independent judgment; to James it was a babble of voices, and he turned to his intimates for advice which he could understand.

The size of the council was greatly increased, and this proved detrimental in certain ways. The council under the Tudors had averaged about twenty members, and certainly its increase under Edward VI and Mary had been coeval with a decline in strength. James at his accession retained Elizabeth's council, which numbered fifteen, and increased it somewhat, partly by the inclusion of several Scots. In May, 1603, the council's membership stood at twenty-four. James said that he regarded this number as too large and gradually reduced it to nineteen or twenty members in 1610. But by 1615 membership had again risen to twenty-four and henceforth it steadily increased. It stood at thirty-one in 1618 and at approximately thirty-five in the period from 1620 to 1625. Charles at his accession reduced the council to some thirty members, but then increased it until in 1630 membership reached forty or just below. It was later reduced somewhat, decreasing to thirty-two in 1635 but rising again to thirty-seven in 1639. Increased membership doubtless did something to lower efficiency. But this may easily be exaggerated. It was a rare occasion indeed when the entire council met together; a meeting with half the council present was a well-attended session, and the average attendance fell far below that figure. Efficiency suffered less from the size than from

fluctuations in attendance; for often the members attending one meeting differed radically in personnel from those attending the next. A much graver result of enlarging the council was the increased difficulty of maintaining secrecy. There was a disastrous leakage of important information from the council under James. The Spanish faction kept Gondomar informed of what went on; and the Venetian ambassador wrote in 1622 that "the king could not utter a thing without the Spanish ambassador, Gondomar, knowing, who was undoubtedly more minutely and profoundly advised than his Majesty." But if James was betrayed by his councillors, he set them a very bad example: it was said that he told Gondomar things he heard from other ambassadors, with the result that foreign princes withheld information from him.

The difficulty in keeping official secrets illustrates the lowered tone of political morality in the early Stuart period. The atmosphere of James's court was venal and mercenary; and as a result the council suffered in both efficiency and reputation. It is not surprising that rapacious courtiers abused James's indulgence to bleed the public or that the Howards accepted Spanish pensions. But one is startled to find that Salisbury also accepted Spanish money and that Bacon received presents from litigants whose cases were pending in his court. The whole system of remuneration for high office was bad. In the middle ages ministers had been rewarded by gifts and grants from the crown; now they received comparatively little from that source and were expected to derive an income from those individuals with whom they dealt in the course of their official duties. But it was often difficult to distinguish a legitimate gift from a payment that was of the nature of a bribe. James accepted the situation with surprising equanimity. He was shaken by the discovery of the Spanish pensions, but the storm blew over without the thorough house cleaning that was called for. He apparently assumed that the more his ministers got from other sources, the less he would have to give them himself; and when they asked him whether they might accept presents offered to them, he told them to do so.

These things cannot be dissociated from the position of the council in the house of commons. Councillors represented kings who were failures and an institution that was falling into rapid decay.

The Realities of Charles I's Personal Rule

CICELY V. WEDGWOOD

Miss Wedgwood (born 1910) has spent her life as a professional writer, principally of history and biography. Her period has always been the late sixteenth and early seventeenth centuries. Her biographies of Strafford and William the Silent are noteworthy. The excerpts in this collection are taken from the first two volumes of what will be a very full *History of the Great Rebellion.*

THE King controlled the appointment of Judges, but he could not control the operation of the law: the machine had a life of its own. At the Assizes the King's Judges instructed the local justices of the peace on the royal policy, issued general recommendations for the future and reprimanded them when the King's policy had not been properly carried out. But in the last resort the King's commands were obeyed only if the justices wanted them to be obeyed; and no effective means existed whereby the justices could be coerced into carrying out any measure which was generally unpopular. The King's council could prosecute, reprimand or remove a few recalcitrant justices but if the majority were to oppose him he could not reprimand or remove the entire bench; who, then, would be left to carry on the necessary affairs of the countryside?

Queen Elizabeth had kept her justices in salutary fear of the royal authority by calling the incompetent before the council; but her fingers were on the pulse of the country and she had avoided collision with public opinion. In this way she had created and maintained a delicate equilibrium between the authority of the Crown and the demands of the subject. She had been respected and feared, but she had also been popular, and she had never allowed any crisis to arise in which her power was pitted against the will of her justices or her people.

King Charles had too high an opinion of the Crown's authority to consider the necessity of maintaining this equilibrium. At the outset of his non-Parliamentary rule he had determined, wisely enough, to bring the justices into regular contact with the Crown by requiring them to make semi-annual reports to the royal council. This plan for more regular and stricter control had coincided with a number of interesting royal proclamations designed to improve the administration of the Poor Law, to prevent the spread of epidemics, to avert famine or a shortage of corn, to control unhealthy and ill-considered building and to relieve the distress of debtors or the chronically disabled. This double move foreshadowed what might have been a benevolent social policy directed and controlled by the Crown, and intended to increase the central power of the King's council at the expense of local and parish authorities.

But the success of the experiment depended on the vigour with which it was prosecuted. After a year or two the social legislation ceased, the proclamations were neglected and surveillance flagged. When, for instance, the King attempted to relieve distress among cloth workers by a government scheme for buying in raw wool and distributing it to the spinners and weavers in each district, it was found that the central government lacked the administrative skill, the authority and the expert knowledge either to compel or to persuade the full co-operation of the justices. The misconceived scheme was allowed to drop but it damaged the prestige of the central government and strengthened, in the justices of the peace, feelings of resentment and contempt.

Although administration thus eluded the King's control, he was still the fountain of justice. He exercised, through the Privy Council and through his Court of Chancery, the power to rectify the errors of any court in the realm, and the errors were many.

High costs and corruption were the prevalent diseases of the courts. Lawyers had their fees and documents cost money; every Court swarmed with hangers-on, clerks, copyists, doorkeepers, each expecting something for his pains, each ready to give extra assistance to the litigant who paid him most, and to do an ill turn to the litigant who forgot to pay him at all. Round Lincoln's Inn and the Temple false witnesses hung about for hire. Suits could be endlessly delayed by the ingenuity or malice of clerks bribed for this purpose, and the delay might be as bad as loss. No one doubted that a rich and powerful man could win a case against a poor man, if by no other means than by spinning it out until his opponent fell into debt and cried for mercy. The

deliberate ruining of some unhappy victim by this means was a frequent subject of contemporary plays, and surviving records give examples of it. Vindictive and false prosecutions occurred; a great landowner might have half the justices of a county in his pocket. Most of those in authority took bribes and, according to the Venetian ambassador who was shocked at the practice, regarded it as harmless and natural.

The law remained popular and serviceable in spite of all. The majority of cases before the courts were not between ill-matched litigants, nor did every powerful man in England abuse his power. For the most part, cases were between equals, where the difference between a fourpenny or a sixpenny bribe did not grossly affect the scales of justice. Corruption, intimidation and general dishonesty were held in check by the practical conviction that, within certain limits, the law must be made to work.

When so much was known to be amiss with the ordinary courts of the realm, the King might have strengthened his position and undermined the influence of the common law by demonstrating the superiority of justice directly dispensed by the Crown. He did not take this opportunity. Widespread as was criticism of the ordinary courts of justice, few if any were heard to praise the superior honesty, speed and cheapness of those directly controlled by the King.

The Court of Chancery, which existed specifically to give a remedy to the subject when there was no remedy at Common Law, was at this time admittedly the most expensive, slow and corrupt court in the Kingdom, and was used quite as frequently as any other court in the realm to forward the interests of the great, more especially those with influence in the royal circle, against those whom they wished to weaken or ruin. The Court of Wards, for several generations the most unpopular court in the Kingdom, was feared and hated by the gentry because it had insensibly become nothing but a means of raising revenue for the Crown at the expense of any estate inherited by a minor, any disputed will or inheritance. Both these courts were famous for interminable and expensive delays, for the number of their predatory clerks and their extortionate charges.

The reputation of the King's Court of Star Chamber, the most important of the prerogative courts, was better, although it was not free of taint. The Star Chamber was simply the King's inner council, with the two Chief Justices in addition, acting as a court of law. The Council's functions had been developed in this way since the time of Henry VII for the express purpose of defending the King's humbler subjects against the unscrupulous powerful. The Star Chamber could and did punish bribery and intimidation; it intervened to stop the deliberate persecution of a small man by a wealthy enemy in the law courts; it called incompetent country justices to order. For more than a century it had held in check the bribing nobleman or the corrupt magistrate who flouted justice too outrageously. But a court created to check abuses had developed abuses of its own, and malicious prosecutions in the Star Chamber were not unknown. King Charles, moreover, had used it to silence critics of the Court, Church or government, and, on occasion, critics or libellers of his friends and ministers. Intending to make his subjects fear his authority, he had in a few cases authorised very heavy fines and humiliating punishments. His subjects were not intimidated; they lost faith in the Star Chamber as a source of protection and became suspicious of it.

Three other courts depended on the King's council: the Court of the North at York, the Court of Wales and the Marches at Ludlow, and the Court of Castle Chamber in Dublin. These too were designed to extend the punitive and protective powers of the King to the furthest parts of his dominions, and to open for the subject a direct path to the justice of his Sovereign or his Sovereign's immediate Deputy. Placed in York, Ludlow and Dublin, they were intended to give the Lord President of the North, the Lord President of Wales and the Marches, and the Lord Deputy of Ireland the necessary powers to control the pretensions and possible violence of the over-mighty lords who in these remoter regions might overawe and oppress His Majesty's lesser subjects. Of the three the Court of Wales had the least to do and was the least criticised. It performed its functions effectively under the mild and pompous guidance of the Earl of Bridgewater whose chief concern was to keep clear of political quarrels. The Lord President of the North and the Lord Deputy of Ireland was one and the same man, the Viscount Wentworth, a governor of a sterner vision than Bridgewater, and facing both in the North and in Ireland a harder task. He had striven manfully to combine the defence of the humble against the mighty with the disciplining of the King's critics. In York, and more especially in Dublin, Wentworth, in case after case, had defended the interests of this or that inarticulate farmer or weeping widow against the tyranny and dishonesty of the great landowners. In Ireland at least, the King's justice had gained with the smaller men a popular reputation for speed and incorruptibility. But in England the benefits Wentworth had bestowed were disregarded, and the severity with which he had punished his opponents was common talk. Sometimes, and not always on the happiest occasions, these Courts worked together. Wentworth had, for instance, condemned a man named Esmond in Dublin; Esmond died soon after, and some of Wentworth's enemies put it about that he died from the after-effects of a blow struck by Wentworth's own vice-regal hand. To crush this libel Wentworth prosecuted the scandalmongers in the Star Chamber. The malicious or ill-informed at once suspected that the Court of Star Chamber was being used to cover the tyrannies committed in Dublin.

The worst characteristics of the prerogative courts was that they encouraged informers and were by no means always competent to distinguish between false information and true; the innocent might be wrecked in the Star Chamber as well as the guilty. Certainly of late years high words at the village pump or a quarrel in an alehouse could, through the malice of an informer, bring a frightened victim before the Star Chamber: Will Brown heard Tom Smith say, "Let the King be hanged" but Tom Smith says he said "You be hanged" and no word concerning the King's Majesty. And so on and so forth, until a sensible justice at Ipswich reporting the case of Ann Dixon, aged fourteen, accused of treasonous words by a neighbour, remarked that if informers continued at this rate every scold's quarrel in the land would come up before the King's council.

Another recent development aroused criticism both in lay and legal circles. The ecclesiastical Court of High Commission had begun to act in very close co-operation with the Court of Star Chamber; they sometimes appeared to function as the spiritual and temporal arms of the same fierce justice. When Dr. Alexander Leighton wrote a virulent attack on the bishops, the Court of High Commission unfrocked him, but the Court of Star Chamber had him flogged and imprisoned for life.

In an age when branding and whipping were common punishments, the prerogative courts had no monopoly of cruelty, but public opinion distinguished very clearly between permissible and impermissible barbarity in criminal sentences: in that steadfastly hierarchic society much depended on the social position of the victim. It was strongly felt that lawyers, physicians and clergymen, persons of university education, who wore black gowns, clean linen, hats, cloaks and gloves, and wrote "gent" after their names, ought not to be subjected to the physical punishments reserved for screeching harlots or drunken vagabonds. The Court of Star Chamber, occasionally, passed such inappropriate sentences and half a dozen of them over as many years were enough thoroughly to perturb the conventional. When the public executioner,

making ready to apply the lash, politely addressed his victim as "Sir," it was evident that a very singular situation had arisen.

The prerogative courts had one other sinister peculiarity. In England torture was unknown to the Common Law; its application was the King's prerogative. As the distinguished lawyer John Selden reflectively remarked: "The rack is nowhere used as in England. In other countries 'tis used in judicature, when there is a *semiplena probatio,* a half-proof against a man: then, to see if they can make it full, they rack him if he will not confess. But here in England they take a man and rack him, I do not know why nor when: not in time of judicature, but when somebody bids." "Somebody" was one of the King's councillors, using the royal authority to apply the torture. King James had used it several times, King Charles only once — unfortunately on an innocent man.

Had the King made the prerogative courts the object of respect, had he asserted a watchful control over the justices of the peace, he would have gone a long way towards making his vision of authority into a reality. But he lacked concentration of purpose. He was too often deflected by immediate considerations of convenience or profit. He had been on the throne twelve years, seven of them without either Parliaments or wars to distract him, yet it was evident to any perceptive observer that he had neither won popular favour for his government nor built up enough strength for himself to make that favour unnecessary.

The reason for this mismanagement — or, more exactly, absence of management — was to be found at the centre of the administration. To help him to realise his vision, the King had need of such ministers as Elizabeth had had — wise, wary, judicious and vigilant, single-minded in their devotion to the task of government. But the very core of King Charles's government, his own council, was feeble, factious and corrupt.

The central government of England was discharged by the King's council, chiefly by

an inner group with no official title although it was sometimes referred to as the
Junto or the Cabinet. At moments of crisis,
or on special occasions — when the Lord
Deputy of Ireland came to report on his
government — the King presided; at ordinary times he rarely attended. As the
council consisted of men who were constantly about the court or held important
offices in the Royal Household, it was easy
for him to consult with individual advisers
at any convenient moment, and since ultimate decisions rested with him alone, the
most important were often taken in private.

The council was essentially a council of
courtiers. Little attempt was made to find
the most experienced man for any special
task or to make use of his ability; the King
preferred to choose from his friends and
servants those who were most congenial to
him, in the ill-grounded belief that he
would find in them the knowledge and
technical skill that was wanted. The principal members of this almost fortuitous group
of noblemen and court officials were few
of them remarkable. There was William
Cecil, Earl of Salisbury; one of the least
distinguished men of a distinguished family, he had a reputation for caution and
parsimony and for having no will of his
own. There was Philip Herbert, Earl of
Pembroke, who concealed his natural crafti-
ness under a mask of buffoonery; he was a
bad-tempered, overbearing man who swore
"God damn me" and boasted of being illiterate — a singular figure in that cultured
society; he retained the King's favour partly
because he could offer him the best hunting
in England, partly because his eccentric
pose appealed to Charles's slow-moving
sense of humour, and chiefly because as a
youth he had been a favourite of the late
King James. Charles was always good to
those whom his father had loved. Another
of his councillors, who had risen in the
same way, was Henry Rich, Earl of
Holland, whose flashing dark eyes and
glossy black hair had earned him the nick-
name of *El Conde*. Vapid, vain and silly,
his thoughts were mostly of dress and of
past and future conquests in the lists of
love, but under a surface charm he was
stubborn, arrogant and vindictive. Holland
was younger brother to the Earl of Warwick, the Puritan pirate and the most
prominent of the lords in opposition to the
Court. Although he resembled his energetic
and capable brother in very little, he was
known to further his brother's interests
whenever he could, which did not make
him a disinterested counsellor for the King.
By comparison with these three the Earl of
Northumberland stands out for his intelligence; his letters show him to have been a
man of reasonably shrewd observation and
judgment, and he had enough knowledge
of naval affairs to acquit himself creditably
in the office of Lord High Admiral.

Two Scots lords also sat on this English
council, the Marquis of Hamilton and the
Duke of Lennox. Hamilton, a favourite
with the King from boyhood, had a kind of
slow-witted cunning and more confidence
in his own judgment than it deserved. The
character of Lennox can be read from
Anthony Van Dyck's different versions of
his fair, aristocratic, equine features: he was
a good young man, loyal, sweet-natured and
simple-hearted, but not clever.

The Treasurer was William Juxon,
Bishop of London, an urbane prelate and
a very upright man. The Chancellor of the
Exchequer was Francis, Lord Cottington,
an irresponsible, irrepressible good fellow,
with a shrewd head, a witty tongue and
few moral scruples; a man whom everybody
liked and no one altogether trusted. There
were two secretaries of state; plodding old
John Coke, honest, painstaking and slow,
but quite incapable of checking the corruption of his clerks, and the lively Francis
Windebanke, with a finger in every intrigue and a family of up-and-coming sons
to place in the world. As makeweight there
was the Comptroller of the Household, Sir
Harry Vane, a jaunty little man bursting
with personal ambition and his own importance.

Holland, Hamilton, Cottington, Windebanke and Vane were all, by taste and

temperament, schemers who used their influence to get profitable places for themselves, their families and friends. The Queen, whose busy and gay nature overflowed easily into such petty conspiracies, encouraged them, and they found other willing friends in the many idle courtiers. Lord Northumberland was not himself a natural plotter, but he had for brother and sister a pair of notable intriguers, Harry Percy, and the beautiful Countess of Carlisle, the Queen's closest friend. The King had friends no less dangerous: his two most trusted Gentlemen of the Bedchamber, Will Murray and Endymion Porter — Dim to his friends — were inveterate wire-pullers. Through these people and their like the council became the heart and centre of Court intrigues rather than the heart and centre of government.

The King's council in England had its exact parallels in Scotland and Ireland. In Ireland it was under the control of the King's Viceroy, the Lord Deputy, who being a strong man and an energetic ruler guided it pretty well as he pleased. Scotland had no Viceroy; the King governed his native country direct from England, but he governed it personally with no reference to his English council which, naturally, had no right to meddle in the affairs of the other nation. The King's Council for Scotland was too far away for the King to be able to discuss matters with them in any effective manner. The connecting link was the Secretary of State for Scotland, Lord Stirling, who followed the Court and communicated the royal wishes to the council at Edinburgh. Their task was mainly to carry out those wishes. King James had developed this peculiar form of government. "Here I sit and govern Scotland with my pen," he had remarked with satisfaction, but he had been able to do so only because by twenty years of astute intrigue and policy he had reduced Scotland to a state of unprecedented docility. In his son's time this was no longer so. What counted in Scottish administration was the authority of Highland chiefs and southern lords and lairds;

early in the century the English system of justices of the peace had been introduced, but it had done no more than confirm the authority already wielded by these men. What counted in Scottish Law was the opinion and influence of the judges, the Lords of Session. King James's Council had represented their interests, made use of their opinions and commanded their respect.

King Charles's Council did none of these things. In the attempt to make it more amenable to his will he had eliminated the Lords of Session altogether from the board and when vacancies were to be filled, he would pass over the great and powerful nobles and place on the Council instead lesser men, in the belief that they would serve him more obediently. It was only a matter of time until he should discover that the authority he exercised through his Council in Scotland had ceased to be any authority at all.

The Scottish Councillors had fewer opportunities for corruption and intrigue than their English counterparts, though they used all that they had, and Lord Traquair the Treasurer was generally regarded as having made a fair part of his fortune out of his office.

The councillors in both countries were open to a certain moral corruption not wholly of their own seeking. Counciliar government in their time was midway between modern cabinet government and the personal system of the Tudors. A modern minister who finds himself in disagreement with government policy resigns his place. A Tudor minister who persistently disagreed with the sovereign's policy would not long have remained in his (or her) confidence. The position of several of King Charles's ministers, both in Scotland and in England, was not only unprecedented but unique in the history of the British Isles. Their advice and opinions were systematically overruled or disregarded by the King, but he kept them in his council and expected them loyally to support and carry out his policy. They could not resign because resignation from the King's Council would have been tantamount to self-inflicted political disgrace. Men like Northumberland in England and Lord Lorne in Scotland were therefore compelled to serve, although it grew yearly more difficult for them to serve with sincerity, honour or loyalty.

The King's two most intelligent ministers, the Archbishop of Canterbury and the Lord Deputy of Ireland, stand out head and shoulders above their corrupt or feeble colleagues and were singleminded in their devotion to the King's ideals. But Charles was as much inclined to pass over their advice as he was that of lesser men.

He supported the Archbishop in his plans for the Church but in most other spheres he resented his interference. Laud was greatly disliked by the Queen and, as if to make up to his wife for his partiality to the Archbishop's views on the Anglican Church, the King opposed him on almost all other matters. He went clean against his advice, for instance, in the favour he showed to Roman Catholics, and was disposed to be irritable when Laud drew his attention to the more difficult and problematical aspects of his home policy. After one discouraging effort to explain to his master certain worrying aspects of the political situation, Laud lamented to his friend the Deputy of Ireland, "The King is more willing *not* to hear than to hear."

The Lord Deputy of Ireland, the King's only other outstanding adviser, owed his position largely to the Archbishop's penetrating judgment. It was probably Laud who had persuaded Charles to offer a seat on the council and a title to one of the most troublesome members of the House of Commons in the Parliament of 1628. Laud had seen that the fervour which moved Thomas Wentworth to oppose the King was a fervour for good government rather than a factious resentment of royal authority. The offer had been accepted, and the leader of an angry House of Commons had been transformed into the most zealous of the King's servants.

Wentworth was a tall, spare, formidable Yorkshireman, with a notoriously bad temper and no personal charm. His dictatorial manner, which reflected his sense of his own position, generally inspired dislike, but he had strong and tender affections and depths of simple loyalty and gratitude in his nature which made him truly beloved by those who knew him best. As a practical administrator he had done well in the North of England, and more than well in Ireland. He was efficient, just and fearless, and he worked with a violent methodical energy at every task he took in hand. Like the King, like Laud, he believed in the establishment of unquestioned authority as the foundation of good government.

Charles, Laud and Wentworth had each of them the desire, and, acting together would have had the skill, to make a reality of that ideal vision of authoritarian government pictured by Rubens or set forth in the masques at Whitehall. But the King wanted the thing done without the strenuous effort of doing it; he deflected the energy and discouraged the efforts of his two best ministers, and believed that he had mastered the problems of the political situation when he had done no more than postpone their solution. He was encouraged in this delusion by optimistic, flattering or ignorant voices at Court, and he became, as each peaceful year went by, ever more willing to be deceived.

The friendship of Laud and Wentworth was cemented by their common frustration. Both were deeply loyal to the King, but critical of his behaviour. In their lengthy correspondence each detailed to the other his views on the events of the day and deplored the intrigues of Court and Council. These letters reveal in both Laud and Wentworth a grasp of essentials, an analytical sense of the situation and a sharpness of judgment which are impressive. The alliance of the two, had it ever become effective, would have given the King's government the strength it so gravely needed. But Charles, following an old, sly, unwise maxim of his father's, did not care to encourage men who were stronger than he.

The King was serious-minded, but he was not industrious. His gravity of manner, and the solemn character of many of his pleasures, have done much to conceal the disarmingly simple truth that he was lazy in all matters of government. His casual attitude to his council, his unwillingness to listen to disturbing information, his hunting three or four times a week, the long hours spent in pursuit or enjoyment of works of art, or in theological discussion — all tell the same tale: he was not interested in practical administration. He idled away the opportunities of his reign, while his two ablest ministers — Laud confined to Church matters only and Wentworth virtually in exile — exchanged their troubled letters, and the rest of his ill-chosen councillors concealed from him anything likely to disturb his equanimity and played at pitch-and-toss with the reputation and resources of the Crown.

The reputation of the Crown was deeply involved with its resources because the measures taken to increase the royal revenues were a principal reason for the dwindling respect in which the government was held. A constant need for money hampered and deformed the King's policy, and the methods he chose to raise it were unpopular and corrupt.

The Ideal of a Balanced Constitution

MARGARET A. JUDSON

Margaret A. Judson (born 1899) was trained at Mount Holyoke and Radcliffe. She is now Professor of History at Douglass College, Rutgers University. Although not everyone would agree with her conclusions, Miss Judson's book represents the most serious attempt to discover, from the sources, exactly what ordinary politicians and lawyers said from day to day, about the nature of English government.

I n the early part of the seventeenth century, men agreed that the king was God's anointed, His vicar or lieutenant on earth, responsible for administering divine justice to man. This belief was proclaimed most often and most eloquently by Anglican preachers, but it was also set forth by lawyers and by leaders of the parliamentary opposition. The judge Sir Henry Finch, in his *Law, or a Discourse Thereof*, wrote as follows: "The king is the head of the commonwealth, immediate under God. And therefore carrying God's stamp and mark among men, and being as one may say, a God upon earth, as God is a king in heaven, hath a shadow of the excellencies that are in God, in a similitudinary sort given him." Lambard, in his *Archeion*, said that the king "is within his owne Kingdome the Vice-roy of God." Another lawyer, giving a charge to the assize held at Norwich, August 4, 1606, said that James "is over us the Lords anointed, and in these his Realms and Dominions, in all Causes, and over all Persons, as well Ecclesiasticall as Civile, next under Christ Jesus our supreame Gouvernour." Twenty-two years later in parliament the same lawyer expressed a similar sentiment concerning Charles when he remarked that "trust in him is all the

From Margaret A. Judson, *The Crisis of the Constitution* (New Brunswick, N. J., 1949), pp. 17–18, 19, 20–21, 22–5, 26–8, 29–33, 34, 35–6, 41–2, 61–2. By permission of the Rutgers University Press.

confidence wee have under God, hee is God's leiuetenant." The lawyer, referring to both James and Charles as God's lieutenant, was Sir Edward Coke.

Right up to the moment when the civil war broke out, the leaders of the parliamentary opposition and Puritan preachers joined with royalist supporters and Anglican clergy in proclaiming the divine origin and sanction of kingly authority and the superiority of the monarchical form of government to all other forms. The parliamentary opposition did not talk of resistance until 1642, and at that late date they insisted they were not resisting the person of the king.

It is essential in understanding the constitutional and political thinking of Englishmen in the early seventeenth century to realize that most of them believed in the divine origin and right of kingly authority; but it is equally necessary to understand that the great majority of them also believed that the king's authority was limited in many ways by the law, the constitution, and the consent of man. To believe in both the divine right of kingly authority and at the same time in its limited nature was perfectly natural and consistent for many excellent seventeenth-century minds.

A second concept concerning the king's authority which almost all men agreed upon at this time was the belief that God, who ordained and established the king, bestowed upon him grace sufficient for his task. To govern was not essentially to wield naked or veiled power, but to practice an art for which a king was peculiarly and uniquely endowed by God. Samuel Daniel wrote of James:

But God, that rais'd thee up to act this parte,
Hath given thee all those powers of worthines,
Fit for so great a worke, and fram'd thy heart
Discernable in all apparences;
Taught thee to know the world, and this great Art
Of ord'ring men, Knowledge of Knowledges;
That from thee men might reckon how this State
Became restor'd, and was made fortunate.

Because men believed that God had ordained kings and endowed them with the art of ruling, they also believed that kings were responsible for doing God's will in the land — for ruling with justice and also with mercy. The king's commands "ought to be just," the speaker said in parliament in 1604, "for he sitteth in the Judgment Seat of the absolute King of Justice." Patricke Scot in his *Table Book for Princes* discoursed at length upon the same question:

The Princely distribution of justice is nothing else but *suum cuique tribuere* [to guarantee to each man his own], is the helme of government, the happinesse of kings and people. From Justice ariseth religion, peace, truth, innocency and true friendship: in it Princes are to bee noble, judicious, grave, severe, inexorable, powerfull and full of majestie; neither enclining to the right or the left hand, to the rich or poore, but determining all matters under their censure, as they looke to be judged by that supreame Judge whose Lieutenants they are.

The unanimity of opinion among Englishmen on the greatness and divine responsibility of their king was not confined to general statements upon the nature of his authority, but also prevailed in considerable measure whenever the question of his particular prerogatives arose.

For purposes of the discussion, it is helpful to divide the king's prerogative in the early seventeenth century into three categories: (1) the special privileges accorded the king in the law courts; (2) his prerogatives as chief feudal lord in the kingdom; (3) his prerogatives as head of the government in the commonwealth.

Protagonists in the seventeenth-century constitutional struggles were not concerned with prerogatives in the first category. No one seems to have questioned these legal privileges. Illustrative of such prerogatives was the important one that the property rights of the king could not be prejudiced in the law courts by the mistake of a subordinate official or by the oversight of a clerk. Neither was the king tied in time.

Prescription did not run against him. There was valid reason why the law favored the king, granting him these special privileges. According to Sir Edward Coke, the king possessed some of his prerogatives because his time and energy were spent on important public business, and according to Hobart, because he studied the art of ruling, the greatest of all arts, and was "intended to consider *ardua regni pro bono publica* [labors of state for the common good]."

A second group of prerogatives of the king consisted of his feudal rights and those obligations due to him as the chief feudal lord in the kingdom. Although Tudor kings had cut deep into the feudal rights of important subjects, they had clung tenaciously to their own feudal rights. In the face of rising expenses and reduced revenues neither James nor Charles had any intention of parting, except for a significant consideration, with any of the feudal rights which had long provided part of the revenue of the English king. By the seventeenth century these feudal prerogatives had become extremely annoying and burdensome to the king's subjects, but desirous as many members of parliament were of getting rid of them, in the debates on the question in 1610 they accepted the fact that these feudal rights belonged to the king, and that their freedom from them could only be obtained by a Great Contract with him.

The most extensive and controversial prerogatives of the king were those connected with his position as head of the state. In that capacity he made the important appointments to the council, the law courts, other departments of state, and to the church. As head of the state he summoned and dismissed parliament at his pleasure. Prerogatives of this sort were seldom mentioned in the law courts and, when they were, never denied. They came to be discussed and eventually questioned and challenged in parliament, but they were not directly attacked there until 1641 and 1642. When at that time some members of parliament worked to take away these particular prerogatives from the king and transfer them to parliament, the civil war soon broke out.

In the years leading up to that war, men agreed also that the king as head of the state was peculiarly competent and solely responsible in certain realms they called government. Here he was most particularly the head of the state, practicing the art of government, a craft possessed only by kings. Within these realms his authority was accepted as absolute. It must be, they believed, or else he would be unable to carry on his craft as a true artist. These realms of government within which his authority was accepted as absolute included foreign policy, questions of war and peace, the coinage, and the control of industries and supplies necessary for the defence of the realm. These matters had been included within the realm called government in the Middle Ages, and had been regarded as peculiarly the king's concern and responsibility. His actions within this special realm had been accepted as absolute, but nevertheless it was believed that such actions could not and did not affect the realm of property within which subjects as well as kings had an interest.

As the constitutional difficulties sharpened in the seventeenth century, each of the spheres formerly accepted as coming under the king's absolute authority as head of the state became a disputed issue between loyal supporters of the king and his parliamentary opponents. It is very striking, however, that most of the leaders in the struggle against the king accepted for a surprisingly long time the absolute power of the king within certain realms. As late as 1621 Coke said: "I will not meddle with the king's prerogative, which is twofold: 1, absolute, to make war, coin money, etc.: 2, or in things that concern *meum et tuum* [mine and thine — legal jargon for "property."], and this may be disputed of in courts of parliament." In the great debate taking place on foreign affairs in the 1621 parliament, the secretary presented a typical view of the king's prerogative in foreign affairs. "Methinks it's a very strange thing for a king to consult with his subjects what war he means to undertake. This were the means for his enemies to know what he intends to do." Phelips replied, revealing, in spite of his boldness, that he recognized the subject was encroaching upon the sphere of the king. Phelips was a leader in advancing the claim of parliament to discuss foreign affairs, but he proceeded carefully, either by means of petitioning the king or by invoking the money-granting power of parliament.

Other bold spirits were equally cautious and confined their demands within regular channels of procedure. Crew argued in the following way. "To make war and peace, to coin, to marry the prince, they are all prerogatives royal; yet in the marriage of the king's son we have all an interest yet we claim no right in it, but only petition for it." In one of the arguments, Delbridge said, "Let us petition and petition again as we usually do to God and without ceasing till he hear us." In a debate on foreign affairs in the 1624 parliament Alford remarked, "Whatsoever we do the king is free. . . ." In the 1628 parliament, Sherland, one of the most zealous supporters of the parliament's cause, said: "The kinge may make warr, may make peace, call parliaments, and dissolve them, these are of the highest nature, for there the king is the *lex loquens* [the speaking law]." Even Oliver St. John, who defended Hampden in the ship-money case, paid lip-service to the concept that the king's power was absolute within certain realms; "in this business of defence," he said, "the *suprema potestas* [the supreme power] is inherent in his majesty, as part of his crown and kingly dignity." When finally in 1642, in the debates over the militia bill, parliament openly claimed control of the defense of the kingdom, this denial of a prerogative long associated with the king helped to precipitate the civil war.

There was still another way in which the king possessed a great prerogative as head of the state. He was responsible for its general well-being, for the "preservation of the whole." According to Staunford, the king was "the preserver, nourisher, and defender of all the people; . . . by his great travels, study, and labors, they enjoy not onely their lives, landes and goodes, but all that ever they have besides, in rest, peace, and quietness. . . ." Salisbury explained in parliament in 1610 that "the true [scale] of the King's prerogative was when it had concurrences with the public good." To Sir Julius Caesar, the king was the "generall father," and all his subjects were "his children," while a speaker in parliament referred to him as "*Parens Patriae* [Father of his country]." The preacher John Stoughton compared the king to a fountain. "The Ancients," Stoughton wrote, "were wont to place the Statues of their Kings by Fountaines, intimating they were the Fountaines of good or ill in the Commonwealth, as indeed they are." Mr. Browne said in the commons in 1628 that "the King is our Soveraigne and that his power is for our good without which we cannot live a godly life." In the ship-money case, it was Oliver St. John, the lawyer defending Hampden, and not one of the king's judges, who remarked: "His majesty is concerned in the way and manner of execution of the highest and greatest trust which the law hath reposed in him, the Safety and Preservation of the Kingdom."

The king's prerogative of pardoning was regarded as existing for the public good. "Justice is tyed to Rules," an anonymous person wrote, "and runs in known and certain Channels, his Mercy hath no other bounds or limits but those of his good pleasure. This is a Prerogative left in the Crown not for the Crown's sake but for the People's and t'is one Essential part of our Liberties that the King should be invested with a fullness of power to show Mercy."

Men agreed in these years of controversy that the king was responsible for the general welfare of all, although they came to disagree on the means or channels through which he could exercise that responsibility. They also believed that the king could not truly discharge his great responsibilities unless at times he used his discretion for the welfare of all. That the king needed discretionary power was clearly explained by Lambard:

As in the government of all Common-weales, sundry things doe fall out both in Peace and Warre, that doe require an extraordinarie helpe, and cannot awaite the usuall cure of Common Rule and settled Justice, the which is not performed, but altogether after one sort, and that not without delay of helpe, and dispense of time: So, albeit here within this Realme of England, the most part of Causes in complaint are and ought to be referred to the ordinarie processe and solemne handling of Common Law, and singular distribution of Justice; yet have there alwayes arisen, and there will continually, from time to time, grow some rare matters meet (for just reason) to be reserved to a higher hand, and be left to the aide of absolute Power, and irregular Authoritie.

Such "irregular authority" did not harm the subject, Lambard believed. On the contrary, it existed for his welfare — to enable the king to render justice to all his people. Without it, "the injuriously afflicted [subject would] be deprived of that helpe and remedie, which both the Ordinances of God, the Dutie of a Kingly Judge, and the common Law of Nature and Reeson doe afford unto him."

Chancellor Ellesmere presented penetrating reasons why only the king could safely be trusted with discretionary power. The king, but no lower official, Ellesmere argued, could be fair and objective to all, because only he was so unconcerned with private interests that he could view the whole dispassionately, free from the private desires which sometimes swayed and clouded the judgments of less exalted men. The king's interests were "public and general"; he was not concerned with "private gain." ". . . the King in that he is the Substitute of God (ymediatelie); the father of his people; and the head of the Commonwealth hath by participation with God and with his [sovereignty] a discretion of Judg-ment and feeling of love towarde those over whome he raigneth and proper to himselfe and his place and person. . . ." Because of his office only the king and no lesser person was "capable of generall discretion."

Neither James nor Charles lived up to the high concept of kingship set forth by Ellesmere. Too often they used their discretionary power for their own private interests or those of their personal favorites, with little consideration for the general welfare of all. Nevertheless, Ellesmere, in his remarks, touched upon a fundamental need of government for which no completely satisfactory solution has ever been found — the need for placing discretionary power, without which no government can function effectively, in hands which will use that power for the public good of all. For Ellesmere and most of his countrymen to believe at this time that a king was the safest wielder of such power was natural. In the first place, a king came closest of all men to God, who was perfect justice; and in the second place, it can be argued on valid psychological and sociological grounds that one raised up by virtue of his office as high above others as a king might have greater consideration for the public welfare than one among equals.

As the difficulties between king and subject intensified in the early decades of the seventeenth century, some Englishmen wanted to increase the discretionary power of the king and to use it in new ways and realms, while others worked to reduce it and confine it within such narrow limits that the best king would have found it hard, if not impossible, to provide for the general welfare. When James ascended the English throne, however, most of his subjects would have subscribed to the views of Lambard and Ellesmere on the discretionary power.

In connection with the king's prerogative as head of the state, the term "act" or "matter of state" was frequently used in the first forty years of the seventeenth century. Sometimes this term was used for his special power in certain realms, such as foreign affairs, sometimes for his general-welfare power, and sometimes in reference to his discretionary power. In the departments of state closest to the king, such as privy council and star chamber, the phrase "act" or "matter of state" came to be more and more used for actions and decrees of the government. Such actions and decrees were eventually attacked by the parliamentary opposition, but at times the term "act of state" was used in parliament with no disapproval of it implied. When, for example, in 1625 Sir Robert Cotton discussed the government's foreign policy, he said that in the reign of James "For matters of state, the Council Table held up the fit and ancient dignity." When leaders of the parliamentary opposition insisted upon discussing certain matters of state which the king tried to prevent their considering, many of those leaders freely admitted that a matter of state was not for them to question. "Lett's not with too much curiosity enter into theis things," Wentworth said in 1621. "If it were for matter of State, lett us not question *archana imperii* [secrets of state]. And not like the Burgundians before Paris thinke so many thistles so many lawnes, but go on to owr business and not be diverted."

It is well known that, in the 1621 parliament, Sir Edward Coke argued in favor of the king's possessing the power to commit persons on grounds of state without the reason being given. According to Coke, it was "against the Bookes of the Law, that the Privy Council should be restrained: . . . That it will hinder the finding out of divers Mischiefs both of State and Commonwealth, if the *Mittimus* [the writ consigning a man to prison] must contain the Cause of every Man's Committment." In the debate which followed, Alford, as staunch a parliamentarian as Coke, agreed that he was willing to leave out from the bill "such Matters as concern the Weal of the State." The question of commitment by the king for reasons of state came up again in parliament in 1624 in connection with the first reading of a bill "for the better

securing of the subject from wrongful imprisonment." A proviso was attached that any penalty in the bill for wrongful imprisonment "shall not extend to any commitment made by his Majesty, or 6 of the Privy Council."

By 1628 many parliamentary opponents of the king had become alarmed at the extent to which the privy council was employing acts of state in the regular administration of government and was imprisoning men who refused to comply with such acts. Coke now declared that the opinion he had expressed in 1621 was mistaken. He and a large group of parliament men agreed that the discretionary power of the king in "matters of state" must be restricted, and in the parliament of 1628 they refused to consent either to a statute or a petition of right which included any mention or saving of the discretionary power. It must not be forgotten, however, that until 1628 most Englishmen, including the leaders of the parliamentary opposition, seem to have believed that the king's discretionary power to act for the general welfare was both legal and necessary.

The king "hath a prerogative in all things that are not injurious to the subject." As kings possessed prerogatives, so subjects possessed rights; and these rights, like the king's prerogatives, were part of the law and basic in the constitution.

The most important of these rights were property rights. To protect them was the principal concern of the common law. It was also the chief concern of great English subjects in the sixteenth and early seventeenth centuries. According to the evidence revealed by the law reports and family papers of this time, men in the upper social classes were adding to their landed holdings. In their acquisition of property, parliament helped them by measures, like the Statute of Uses, which made the transfer of property easier than it had ever been before. The crown helped them also by the sale of the confiscated monastic lands. The great mistake of the Tudors if they wished to be despots (as Harrington clearly pointed out in his *Oceana* in 1656) was their encouragement of such measures. It was a mistake from the point of view of the king's position, because, at the same time as the king's authority was increasing in the sixteenth century and the concept of divine right of kings was rising to new exalted heights, the amount of property possessed by influential subjects was also increasing and thereby strengthening the old medieval concept that property was a right belonging to subjects. Among the many reasons why the growing absolutism of the Tudors did not become complete absolutism under the Stuarts is the fact that the medieval concept of the inviolability of a man's property did not disappear or become weaker in the sixteenth or early seventeenth centuries. Tudor and Stuart noblemen, gentry, and merchants who were acquiring property did not forget that although "government belonged to kings, property belonged to subjects."

Men looked to the common law courts to protect their property, and those courts did not fail them. During the same period when the decisions in Bate's case and the ship-money case in favor of the king's prerogative against the subjects' property were rendered, many decisions were handed down and remarks made in the common law courts in favor of the subjects' property — even against a private prerogative or right of the king. In the case of the Duke of Lennox, for example, it was said that the king could not pardon an offender who had not repaired a bridge because the subjects had an "interest" in that bridge which could not be taken away by the king's pardon. Likewise, in the case of *The King v. Boreston and Adams* it was implied that although the king's mercy could pardon a person who had been attainted, his pardoning power could not restore the right to land of such a person because that right was another's and not the king's. Extensive as the king's prerogative was admitted to be for the defense of the realm, it was declared by all the justices in the case of the prerogative of the king in saltpeter that, although

the king's officials might dig for saltpeter, they were "bound to leave the inheritance of the subject in so good a plight as they found it." Another illustration of similar care for the subjects' property occurs in the case of lands acquired by the crown which were subject to certain obligations, as for example, tithes. "It could not be permitted to the Crown to refuse Payment if, by so doing the obligation would be thrown on the other persons."

During the years between 1630 and 1640 the principle that property belonged to the subject was never directly attacked, even though parliament was never in session to guard it. Royalist judges in the ship-money case still accepted in principle the property rights of the subject. The remarks of these men, staunchly upholding the correctness of ship money yet insisting that it was not a tax, are very revealing. Littleton said: "Again, it is not in question, whether the subject hath a property in his goods, or can lose them without consent in Parliament. I shall shew that his property shall remain unto him notwithstanding this assess." Banks remarked that "This writ denieth not the property to be in the subject." Berkeley showed that although this government is monarchical, yet subjects "have in their goods a property, a peculiar interest, a *meum et tuum*"; while Trevor said of the sum assessed, "the subjects are not prejudiced by it, either in their dignities, or properties in their goods."

Most Englishmen not only admitted the sanctity of property but liked to point out that a monarchy respecting the subjects' rights was the highest and truest form of monarchy. England, they were proud to proclaim, was most fortunate in its government. "This Iland," Richard Martin of the Middle Temple told James, "shall never feare the mischiefes and misgovernments, which other countries and other times have felt. Oppression shall not be here the badge of authoritie, nor insolence the marke of greatnesse. The people shall every one sit under his owne Olive tree, and anoint himself with the fat thereof, his face not grinded with extorted sutes, nor his marrow suckt with most odious and unjust Monopolies."

A monarch was regarded as a true monarch if he ruled over free people who showed their love and gratitude to him by voluntary gifts of their own. "It was the greatest Honour of the king to govern Subjects moderately free." The speaker of the commons in 1624 explained that James was under God "a sole and entire Monarch," yet nevertheless parliamentary grants were free. In the words of Archbishop Abbot, "There is a *Meum* and a *Tuum* in Christian Commonwealths, and according to Laws and Customs, Princes may dispose of it, that saying being true *Ad Reges potestas omnium pertinet, ad singulos proprietas* [Power over all things belongs to kings, property belongs to individuals]." A monarch whose authority did not include the right to take his subjects' property was royal, as Bodin had once said. Such a monarch possessed something greater than the mere material wealth of his people — he possessed their love. With their love he did not need to own their property, for they would freely grant it to him for his legitimate needs. A monarchy of this type most truly reflected the divinity and justice of God, who had ordained and exalted the king and given him many prerogatives, but who had also given property to the greatest of his subjects and manual skill to the lowliest, and had provided that neither the subject's property nor his manual skill fell within the realm of the king's authority.

It seems quite clear that in the first part of the seventeenth century councillors, lawyers, judges, and members of parliament recognized, as they carried on the work of government in council, court, and parliament, that an adjustment must often be made between the king's prerogative and the subjects' rights. To them such adjustment was not a medieval survival but a living reality — an indispensable means of preserving the prerogative of the king and the rights of the subjects they held so dear.

As adjustment was a live and necessary part of the functioning of government, so the ideal of balance was one of the most cherished and strongest beliefs Englishmen agreed upon between 1603 and 1640. Late in Elizabeth's reign James Morice gave a picture of the happy balance between king and subject prevailing in England:

Behold with us the Sovereigne Aucthoritie of one, an absolute Prince, Greate in Majestie, rulinge and reigninge, yet guyded and directed by Principles and precepts of Reason, which wee terme the lawe. No Spartane Kinge, or Venetian Duke, but free from accompt and cohersion of anye, eyther equall or Superiour; yet fermilie bound to the Comon wealth by the faithfull Oathe of a Christian Prince, bearinge alone the sharpe Sworde of Justice and Correction, yet tempered with mercy and compassion; requiringe Taxe and Tribute of the people, yet not causelesse, nor without common assent.
We agayne the Subjects of this Kingdome are borne and brought upp in due obedience, butt farre from Servitude and bondage, subject to lawfull aucthoritie and commaundement, but freed from licentious will and tyrannie; enjoyinge by lymitts of lawe and Justice our liefs, lands, goods, and liberties in great peace and security. . . .

This Elizabethan ideal of a balanced government lived on to play an important part in the thinking of men in the early seventeenth century. In their Apology of June 1604 the commons, accepting the prerogatives of princes but recognizing that such prerogatives "may easily and do daily grow," drew up for James the rights and liberties of his new English subjects which were their due inheritance. When these prevail, they told their king, "an harmonical and stable state is framed, each member under the head enjoying that right, and performing that duty, which for the honour of the head and the happiness of the whole is requisite."

Revolutionary Tactics—and Charles I's Decisive Blunder

CICELY V. WEDGWOOD

For the King and for Pym, the war in Ireland was principally a weapon to be wielded in the struggle at home. The centre of conflict was not, for them, in the burning villages of Munster, in threatened Dublin or oppressed Kilkenny. It was at Westminster. Pym had already used the Irish Rebellion to discredit the Court and the Royal Family; though he had been cautious of involving the King, he had repeatedly insinuated that the Queen, her priests and her friends knew more than they should. So now Charles, in his speech to Parliament, used the disasters in Ireland to make his opponents in the Commons appear remiss in assisting the English settlers. The phrasing of this speech and especially the suggestion that the Militia Bill should have a *salvo jure* clause added to it — to safeguard the rights of the King, and thus destroy its whole purpose — seems to have been suggested by Oliver St. John, the Solicitor General. St. John belonged to Pym's party and his appointment earlier in the year had been designed partly to pacify the King's opponents, partly to bribe St. John himself into friendship. He may have made the suggestion in all good faith, but Edward Hyde later thought it had been a trap to enable John Pym to accuse the King of breach of privilege. A reference from the Throne to a bill still under discussion in Parliament was, Pym averred, a grave interference with freedom of debate.

But he was evidently worried by the favourable impression that the King's well-judged words on Ireland might make. The Grand Remonstrance, now three weeks old, had failed of its effect in discrediting Charles because Charles had taken so little notice of it. At dusk on December 15th, when many Royalists had withdrawn (they were still unable to accept the necessity of coming to the House early and staying late), one of Pym's staunchest men, old Sir William Purefoy, the member for Warwick borough, suddenly moved that the Remonstrance be printed. The startled Royalists tried to postpone the motion but were defeated by nearly a hundred votes. They strove next to delay the printing, but although they managed to whip in a few more of their errant supporters in the interim they were again heavily defeated. More welcome to Pym, perhaps, than the vote itself was this evidence that the King's friends were still outmatched by him in the management of Parliamentary business.

His next move was to persuade the Lords that the King's reference to the Militia Bill had been a breach of privilege. This did not prove difficult and the Lords joined with the Commons in a protest to which was added a demand: they desired to know the names of the "evil councillors" who had inspired the speech. In this action, the moderates, hoodwinked as they were by their misplaced confidence in the goodwill of both parties, played a considerable part.

On the day on which Charles received the protest from Parliament, Lord Dillon arrived at Court with his message from the Lords of the Pale. Very soon it was generally reported that Dillon had strongly advised the pacification of Ireland by giving full liberty of conscience to the Roman

Catholics. The report did much to increase suspicion of the King's sympathy with the rebels, and to wipe out the effect of his appeal to Parliament for instant help for the English settlers.

Charles was none the less confident of his growing strength and showed it by the answer which, after three days' delay, he gave to the Parliamentary protest. Summoning the delegation into his royal presence he told them with dignity that he would not reveal the names of his councillors, for this was not a demand to be made to a man of honour. As to breach of privilege, the bill was already in print and he did not see how his reference to it could be accounted a breach; he would always maintain Parliament's lawful privileges, and he hoped they would be as careful to maintain his just prerogatives. This said, he rose and with an air "confident and serene" left them to digest his answer.

The London M. P.'s had been working hard to undermine the authority of the Royalist Lord Mayor, Sir Richard Gurney. Complaints now reached Parliament that he had obstructed the London petition against the Bishops, but there was not matter enough in these to procure his removal, and other means had to be tried to regain control of the much divided City. The Common Council of London was in theory elective; but in practice the same substantial citizens composed it year after year. By a dexterous campaign in favour of new members, Venn and his friends organised a real election and on December 21st succeeded in ousting many of the King's friends from the Common Council and placing on it a number of Puritan-minded citizens, some of humble status — a tailor, a cutter, a dyer, said their contemptuous but defeated opponents, and even one "Riley the squeaking Bodice-maker."

While Pym and his friends made sure of the City, Charles was making sure of the Tower. In the week before Christmas the House of Commons learnt that Sir William Balfour, the Scottish soldier of fortune and rabid Protestant who had long been lieu-

tenant of the Tower, had been compelled by the King to give place to Colonel Thomas Lunsford. Lunsford, whom Pym's party clamorously described as a "very desperate" man, was such another bold and violent swaggerer as had figured among the King's friends in every real or supposed plot of the previous summer. His appointment was by no means pleasing to the King's moderate supporters and one of these, Sir Ralph Hopton, went up to the House of Lords to ask for a joint petition to the King for Lunsford's instant removal.

On the day of the uproar over Lunsford's appointment Charles sent his reasoned answer to the Grand Remonstrance. It had been drafted apparently with no official intention by Edward Hyde, seen by Digby and at once taken over by him to be issued in due course as the official reply to the accusations made against the King. It set forth the concessions which had been made during the last year and went on to outline a policy for the future. The King declared that he would be willing to make certain allowances in matter of religion to those of tender consciences, but the Church of England was none the less "the most pure and agreeable to the Word of God of any religion now practised in the Christian world," and he would, if called upon, seal that belief with his blood. For the rest he desired nothing more than an understanding with Parliament so that he might be a "great and glorious King over a free and happy people." The paper reflected the baseless hopes of the King's group of friends in the House of Commons. They alone would be taken by surprise at each twist in the next fortnight's steep descent to catastrophe.

With the Tower in the King's hands and the Lords divided, the Commons adjourned uneasily for two days over Christmas. They took a shorter holiday than custom permitted to the generality. The twelve days of Christmas from December 25th to January 6th were the habitual span of merry-making, the Christianised Saturnalia against which the Puritans had hitherto protested in vain. This year's Saturnalia was to be a blessed one for them. The apprentices, legitimately on holiday, surged around Whitehall in righteous high spirits shouting "No Bishops," "No Popish Lords," and "Down with butcher Lunsford," until Gurney, still trying to hold the City for the King, implored him to withdraw Lunsford from the Tower. On December 26th Charles substituted Sir John Byron, a man of better reputation no less loyal to himself. Lunsford continued in high favour at Court.

On Monday December 27th Parliament reassembled and Sir William Jephson, a Munster landowner and a kinsman of Pym, reported from Ireland further evidence that the rebels had the Queen's authority to rise for the defence of the Roman Church. Pym followed this statement by reading aloud the official letter from the Lords of the Pale asking for the toleration of Catholicism. He was deliberately fomenting the suspicion raised by Jephson because he wished to force the issue with the King. He intended to threaten, or appear to threaten, the impeachment of the Queen. In the face of such an affront Charles would have to attack, whether or not he was ready. He was not quite ready.

Pym had barely finished speaking when an anxious member — a Royalist this time — warned his colleagues that there was fighting outside in Westminster Hall. Lunsford and some friends, jostled by the apprentices, had lost their tempers and drawn their swords. This time no harm was done, but in the next three days the rioting grew more serious. Down by the river crowds blocked the stairs at Westminster and would not let the Bishops land to take their seats in Parliament. Yelling "No Bishops," "No Popish Lords," they held up coaches in the adjoining streets and, in the grey winter light, thrust torches through the windows to see who was within. Archbishop Williams hit out in unclerical fashion at the impudent rogues, boxed the ears of one and tumbled another underfoot, but the apprentices were too many for him and

he had to be rescued by a brace of Protestant peers and helped into the House of Lords with his tippet torn off. By evening the crowds had grown so thick that the Marquis of Hertford advised no Bishop who had managed to reach the House to venture out again, and Lord Mandeville, for the sake of his old friendship with Williams, smuggled several of them to his nearby lodgings for the night. The rabble next day, finding a leader in the crazy broken-down Sir Richard Wiseman, who had been a Star Chamber victim three years earlier, stormed Westminster Abbey, and were thrown back by some of the King's guards. A falling tile killed Wiseman and sobered them for the time being. The King denounced the rioters, sent to the Lord Mayor to call out the City Trained Bands against them if necessary, and ordered all his courtiers to wear swords for his and their defence.

Sustained by Digby, who was confident that all would be well, the King serenely pursued his plans. On December 29th he entertained Lunsford and his principal officers to a Christmas dinner at Whitehall. As they came out, exhilarated with wine and good company, the apprentices hanging about the palace greeted them with the usual parrot chorus of "No Bishops." For the second time Lunsford flashed out his sword and went for them, and this time there was a serious fight before the boys were driven off leaving some prisoners and wounded behind them. The fame of the battle went round the City and the apprentices gathered angrily in the torch-lit darkness. Even John Venn seems to have been afraid of what they might do and appealed to them not to storm the Lord Mayor's house. Instead, they broke into one of the City prisons before dispersing, exhausted, homewards. During that day the offensive epithets of "Roundhead" and "Cavalier" were for the first time freely bandied about. Roundhead was an easy word of contempt for the shorn, bullet-headed apprentices, but Cavalier, which so soon acquired its gay and gallant associations, had when it was first angrily hurled at the King's men an ugly sound — "cavaliero," "caballero," Spanish trooper — brutal oppressor of Protestants and national enemy.

Next day, December 30th, Archbishop Williams took an unwise step. Digby had already attempted to move, in the House of Lords, that the threats of the rabble invalidated the present sessions of Parliament by infringing the freedom of members. The Lords had quelled this motion because, if the principle were once accepted, it could be extended to invalidate most of the legislation of the previous spring. The Bill of Attainder against Strafford had quite evidently been carried only because of the pressure of the rabble. Archbishop Williams now took up Digby's idea, possibly with his advice and connivance. In hurried consultation with his fellow Bishops he drew up a protest against their forcible exclusion from the House of Lords, implying that in their absence the House was incomplete and its acts of doubtful authority.

The King handed over the document, when it was shown to him, to the Lord Keeper, without troubling to read it — an omission which may have been mere carelessness, though it is equally possible that he knew already from Digby what the document contained. When the Lord Keeper in his turn presented it to the House of Lords, it was very badly received not only by Pym's party but by the House in general, who had already expressed their views on this question when Digby had raised it, and were irritated at having it raised once again. Pym's friends saw to it that he was instantly informed in the Commons of what was happening in the Lords. With the speedy help of the lawyer John Glynne, he got the Commons within half an hour to vote the impeachment of all the bishops who had signed the protest. The Lords, offended and perturbed by this second clumsy attempt to invalidate their sessions, agreed to the impeachment, and a dozen venerable clerics were immediately hustled off to prison "in all the extremity of frost, at eight o'clock in the dark evening." That

night the apprentices rang all the bells of the City and lit bonfires in the street, but the Queen was telling Heenvliet, the Prince of Orange's envoy, that her husband would stand firm. The moment had come.

Each side asserted that the other intended violence. Pym, before he turned on the bishops, had informed a rather mystified House of Commons that some villainous design was plotting against them. The King next day asked the City Trained Bands to stand ready against "the mean and unruly people" who disturbed the peace. But the House of Commons sent Denzil Holles to appeal to the King that these same Trained Bands might guard Parliament against the violence of the "malignant party."

On January 1st, to show that their fears were genuine, the House went into Committee at Guildhall, as they alleged, for safety. Whispers had by this time reached the King — as Pym intended that they should — that the Queen's impeachment was imminent. Charles believed that he had no time to lose. A dank and rainy winter had made the roads difficult, and the additional members of Parliament, on whom he relied to destroy Pym's dominance in the Commons, had not yet reached Westminster. But he thought himself strong enough to act without them, and believed that a greater danger was in delay. First he issued a proclamation denouncing the Irish as traitors, a move designed to stifle the slander which associated him and the Queen with the rebellion. Then he sent Falkland to Pym with an olive branch which he knew very well would be rejected: he offered him the post of Chancellor of the Exchequer. This empty gesture was designed to please the moderates and disarm suspicion. On Pym's refusal he made Culpeper Chancellor of the Exchequer and Falkland Secretary of State.

They were sworn on Sunday, January 2nd. On Monday, January 3rd 1642, the King unmasked his guns and opened the cannonade against Pym and his junto. In the House of Lords, the Attorney General, Sir Edward Herbert, accused of High Trea-

son the six principal men of the party—
Lord Mandeville, John Pym, John Hampden, Arthur Haslerig, Denzil Holles and
William Strode. Digby, who had inspired
the project and advised the moment of
attack, overplayed his part. While Herbert
was speaking, he was so busy whispering
his astonishment to Lord Mandeville and
wondering who could possibly have advised
the King, that he missed his cue. He should
have risen, when Herbert concluded, to
move the instant imprisonment of the
accused men — as the Bishops had been
imprisoned immediately after their impeachment a week earlier. He let the
moment slip, then either lost his nerve or
changed his mind, and hurried from the
House, leaving the Lords stunned and
baffled by the King's new move and with
no one to indicate even to the King's friends
what they should do next.

The House of Commons, apprised of
what went forward almost before Herbert
had concluded, sent in an immediate request for a conference with the Lords,
claiming that the accusation was a breach
of privilege. So also, they asserted, was the
behaviour of the King's officers who had
that morning invaded and searched the
lodgings of Pym and Holles. In the meantime, neither House would yield up the
accused men.

After nightfall two of the City members,
John Venn and Isaac Pennington, urgently
asked the Lord Mayor for a guard from the
London Trained Bands for Parliament lest
the King's soldiers should attack. Gurney
was unresponsive, and about midnight he
was called out of bed by a messenger from
the King forbidding him to send the
Trained Bands to help the House of Commons. Charles added another and ominous
word to the Lord Mayor: should any more
tumults occur, he authorised the City
Trained Bands to fire on the crowd.

The King sent messengers also to the
Inns of Court, bearing the articles of
impeachment against his enemies and a
request to the gentlemen volunteers among
lawyers and law students to stand ready

for the defence of King and Kingdom at
an hour's warning. Charles felt very confident. Sir John Byron was in charge of the
Tower; the guards and gentlemen pensioners about Whitehall were led by the
formidable Lunsford and young Lord Roxburgh who had been so hotly involved in
the Edinburgh "incident" a few months
before; Digby was on his way into Surrey
to collect volunteers with whom he confidently believed he could march on London.
The King did not doubt that Pym's apprentices would collapse before a concerted
attack, and he trusted in the Lord Mayor's
loyalty to prevent the City Trained Bands
from giving help to the wrong side.

It must have been evident to Pym, without more specific warning, that the King
intended to lay hands on him and the other
accused men by force. For the details of
the plan he depended on information from
the Court which reached him sometimes
from Lady Carlisle and sometimes from
Will Murray; but they do not appear to
have known more than was generally
apparent — that the King would strike, but
precisely when, and in what manner, they
could hardly know for he was not yet
certain himself. Pym therefore planned his
answering strategy in the half-dark. He
and his accused friends could have left the
House of Commons and evaded the danger
of a forcible arrest; but it was essential that
the King's violent intention towards Parliament be put beyond doubt. The King
would only attempt an act of violence if
Pym and his colleagues were there to be
seized. The trap must be baited: the Five
Members were the bait.

So the House sat at Westminster, not at
Guildhall, on the morning of January 4th
and all the accused were present. They
must be there until the King's guards were
well on their way to Parliament; but they
must not be there when the guards arrived.
Should they be seized, the King would have
secured his principal objective, whatever
tumults might ensue; their party in Parliament would collapse once they were gone,
and with them the directing power which

made the tumults dangerous. But if they escaped, the King's attempt at violence would be nakedly revealed, and he would have gained nothing by it.

Everything depended on timing. The Commons passed an uneasy morning sending messages to the Lord Mayor and the Inns of Court to counteract those which the King had sent overnight. They adjourned nervously for dinner at noon, and Pym heard, over his meal from his good friend the Earl of Essex, that the King would certainly make his attempt that afternoon. The Commons reassembled at half-past one. Pym counted on the French Ambassador to let him know the movements at Whitehall, and at about three a breathless young Frenchman, Hercule de Langres, came hurrying through the outer Courts of Westminster with the news. The King was coming himself, with his guards about him.

Had Charles succeeded, his act of inspired audacity would have been an object lesson on the might and authority of the Sovereign against the factious subject. But if there was the least risk of failure, the project was folly; the attempt, and not the deed, would confound him utterly. He should not, unless he was acting on an absolute certainty, have taken part in the arrest himself, for by doing so he cut off his own retreat; he would never be able to shift the blame.

As Charles approached from Whitehall, Pym in the Parliament House asked leave of the Speaker for himself and his friends to go. The truculent William Strode, who had already spent ten years of his life in prison for his defiance of the King in earlier Parliaments, held them up with an untimely display of courage; he wished to confront the King and did not understand the more subtle intentions of Pym. There was no time for explanation or argument and his friends dragged him out by his cloak. At the watergate a barge waited, and the Five Members were on their way to the City when Charles came in through Westminster Hall.

The King left his following in the lobby of the House and, accompanied only by his nephew the Elector Palatine, entered the chamber. Roxburgh, negligently propping himself on the door jamb, kept the doors open so that the members could see the troops, some of whom were already cocking their pistols and playfully pretending to mark down their men. Charles, as always meticulous in little things, took off his hat as he entered the House and walked bareheaded towards the Speaker's chair, saluting some of the members as he went. The members, also bareheaded, stood in silence. They saw him look quickly to the right near the bar of the House, where Pym usually sat. "Mr. Speaker," said the King, "I must for a time make bold with your chair." Lenthall made way for him. Charles tersely explained why he had come and then asked for the members by name. "Is Mr. Pym here?" His words fell into a dead silence. Impatiently he asked the Speaker if the five members were present. Lenthall, with an unwonted inspiration, fell on his knees and said that it was not his part either to see or to speak but as the house directed. "'Tis no matter," said the King, "I think my eyes are as good as another's," and in the awful silence he continued to look along the benches "a pretty while" before at last he accepted defeat. "All my birds have flown," he said forlornly, and stepping down from the Speaker's chair, went out, "in a more discontented and angry passion than he came in" — as well he might.

The intended act of strength had failed. Digby that night offered to go into the City with Lunsford and seize the accused men; this Charles refused, but with a desperate tenacity he tried once again. He made Edward Nicholas draw up a proclamation calling on his loyal subjects in London to deliver up the accused men; Littleton, the Lord Keeper, refused to seal it. Charles would not be deflected. He drove into the City. The shops were closed and the streets full of people. A fanatic tossed a paper into the Royal coach headed "To your tents, O Israel"; it was an open cry for rebellion. The Lord Mayor had called the Common

Council but the newly-elected Puritan members, regardless of the custom which fixed their assumption of office as the first Monday after Twelfth Night, crowded in prematurely to the meeting, and the Mayor dared not expel them for fear of worse trouble. The King promised them security of religion, a free Parliament and speedy action against the Irish rebels, but he demanded the persons of the five traitors whom he believed to be hiding in the City. Some cried "Privilege," others, but not many, set up a shout of "God Save the King."

"No privilege can protect a traitor from legal trial," said Charles, and went to dine with the Lord Mayor and Sheriffs. But he knew now that Gurney, loyal though he was, could not answer for the City. He could barely answer for himself and that very evening was set upon by an angry crowd. When Charles drove home in the winter dusk, the people who not six weeks before had cheered him home by torchlight surged round his coach, menacing and insolent, with shouts of "Privilege! Privilege!" Those with the King noticed for the first — and perhaps the only — time in his career that he was unnerved.

He had cause to be. He had lost London. On the next day the House of Commons met in Committee at Guildhall and issued a proclamation denouncing as public enemies any who assisted the King in his attempt to seize its members. (The accused men themselves were snugly in hiding in a house in Coleman Street.) The Common Council, defying the Lord Mayor, drafted a petition against Roman Catholics at Court and Sir John Byron's command at the Tower. It was hourly expected that the King's furious Cavaliers — multiplied by rumour into thousands — would attack the City; apprentices built blockades of benches across the streets; women boiled cauldrons of water ready to pour from the windows, and the Trained Bands mustered in readiness.

At Whitehall the twelfth day of Christmas passed in gloom and disarray. The players presented *The Scornful Lady* to the little Prince of Wales and a sparse unhappy audience. No soldiers marched on the City. No one knew what to do.

The Common Council of London stretched out the right hand of friendship to the fragmentary fugitive Parliament within their gates. They formed themselves into a joint Committee for Public Safety and on Saturday, January 8th, bestowed the freedom of the City on Philip Skippon, a pious professional soldier, veteran of the Dutch wars, to whom on the following Monday Parliament gave the command of the Trained Bands, overruling the protests of the Lord Mayor and disregarding the rights of the King.

The King had never contemplated the failure of the master stroke on which he had counted and planned since he left Scotland. He had felt himself secure in the support of the Lord Mayor, in the gallantry of his soldiers, in the skill of his advisers. The failure left him without policy or goal, at one moment stubborn and indignant, at the next leaning on his moderate friends for support. They, poor men, knew not what to do. Their hopes had collapsed more finally than the King's. It was not for actions of this kind that they had defended his policy and fervidly upheld his authority in Parliament. They hardly dared to attend the sessions of the Commons in the City, and they had lost heart and hope for organising their fellow members for the King. Stunned rather than gratified, Culpeper and Falkland entered on the responsibilities of the offices he had recently thrust upon them.

Hitherto the apprentices and the Trained Bands had shouted loudest for Parliamentary privileges. On Monday, January 10th, the port and the riverside rose. Mariners and lightermen flocked into the City, offering to live and die for Parliament. At any moment now it looked as though all London would spill out towards Westminster to demand justice or blood. This would be no mere uncontrolled thronging rabble — fearful as that could be. The Trained

Bands had been mobilised and stood to their arms, under the able leadership of Philip Skippon; there was marching and drilling in the City, cannon and chains across the streets. The sea-faring Earl of Warwick and young Vane, Treasurer of the Navy, had been at work among the seamen and the river was full of boats, manned and waiting.

Charles hesitated, seeing that to show fear would be to weaken his remaining supporters in London. The Earls of Essex and Holland both argued with him that he should remain at Whitehall at all costs, but he did not trust either of them, knowing their sympathy with his enemies. The Queen told Heenvliet that rebellion had begun. She may have been responsible for making the King take part himself in that rash descent on the House of Commons, and she worked herself into a hysterical belief that her indiscretion alone had betrayed it to Pym. On the night of January 10th, suddenly and improvidently, the Royal pair fled from the capital, taking their three eldest children. They reached a dark and unprepared Hampton Court, late and tired, and slept — King, Queen and three children — all in one bed.

Next day in London, at Three Cranes Wharf, John Pym, John Hampden, Denzil Holles, Arthur Haslerig and William Strode, stepped into a barge to the acclamations of the people. The rest of the members embarked behind them, and the Parliament men were accompanied up the Thames to Westminster by a regatta of decorated craft, of cheering citizens and mariners. With Lord Mandeville in their midst, Skippon and the Trained Bands, drums beating and colours flying, marched down the Strand to rejoin them at Westminster; as they passed the emptied palace of Whitehall they called out "Where is the King and his Cavaliers?" Returning conquerors could have had no more impressive welcome. They were conquerors: they had taken the City of London and driven the King into exile from his own capital. The next time he came to Westminster, he would be a prisoner on trial for his life.

Work Still to Be Done

CHRISTOPHER HILL

THE Puritan Revolution is dead and buried, and I do not want to resurrect it; but need Puritanism be left altogether behind the door? The importance of economic issues has been established; but we still have to find a synthesis which will take cognizance of this and yet give some explanation of why in 1640 not only M. P.'s but a large number of other people thought bishops the main enemy; why there were so many conflicts before 1640 over the appointment of lecturers in town corporations; why, when the troops got drunk on a Saturday night in 1640, their animal spirits were worked off in the destruction of altar rails; why Cromwell's Army marched into battle singing psalms.

The following points, I would suggest, will have to be included in our ultimate synthesis:

(i) A much more serious study needs to be made of the political effects of the

From Christopher Hill, "Recent Interpretations of the Civil War," in *Puritanism and Revolution* (London, 1958), pp. 24–31. By permission of Martin Secker & Warburg, Ltd.

"industrial revolution" of the century before 1640. Professor Nef's valuable suggestions in his *Rise of the British Coal Industry* have not been properly followed up. The struggle over monopolies was not only of financial and constitutional importance; it was also of the greatest consequence for the future of capitalism in industry that there should be freedom of economic development. Further knowledge here might help us to a clearer understanding of the support which towns (except sometimes their ruling oligarchies) and the rural industrial areas gave to the parliamentary cause.

(ii) When Dr. Valerie Pearl's eagerly awaited thesis on the City of London is published, we shall have a clearer picture of politics there in the crucial years 1640–3. We shall know more about the links between the ruling oligarchy of aldermen and the Court, which made the City government Royalist, and isolated it from the majority of the Common Council and of City voters, who were radical Parliamentarians: and about the fierce conflicts which led to the violent overthrow of the royalist clique in the winter of 1641, just in time to make the City a safe refuge for the Five Members. But more work is still needed on London politics after 1643, and on political struggles in other towns.

(iii) We should also, I believe, look more closely at colonial and imperial policies. Since Newton's book we all recognize the crucial importance of the Providence Island Company, but this was after all one of the smaller companies. The full political effect of disputes over colonial questions on the origin and progress of the revolution has never been fully worked out. But when we find the Witney blanket-makers asking the House of Lords in 1641 to protect the rights and privileges of the Royal Africa Company, we can imagine how many people's lives were already affected by freedom of export.

(iv) Professor Campbell and Dr. Hoskins have directed our attention to the rising yeomen; but there has been no full analysis of his economic problems in relation to government policy, nor of those of the small clothiers and artisans generally. Yet traditionally these classes are believed to have formed the backbone of the New Model Army, and most contemporaries agree in putting them solidly on the parliamentary side, at least in the south and east. There is a danger that in riveting our attention on the gentry we may underestimate social groups which were at least of equal importance once the old stable social structure began to crumble, and whose grievances helped to make it crumble.

(v) This brings us to a subject one mentions with diffidence — the people of England. Gardiner and the Whigs often assumed too lightly that Parliament represented "the people," that it is easy to know what "the people" wanted. But the modern tendency is again to throw the baby out with the bath water, and to leave out of account those who actually fought the civil war. Tenants no doubt often turned out to fight as their landlords told them, London demonstrations could be organized, the rank and file of the New Model Army were not all as politically sophisticated as the Agitators. Granting this, the evidence still suggests that in 1640 there was a real popular hostility to the old regime whose depth and intensity needs analysis and explanation, and whose influence on the course of events after 1640 we almost certainly tend to underestimate. The consumers and craftsmen who suffered from the high prices caused by monopolies; the peasants whom Laud's good intentions failed to protect, and who thought the time had come to throw down enclosures in 1640–1; the ordinary citizens who resisted the Laudian attempt to increase tithe payments; the small men for whom the parson of the established church (*any* established church) was "Public Enemy No. 1"; the members of the sectarian congregations of the sixteen-forties and -fifties whose naive but daring speculations have still to be properly studied in their social setting — it was these men, not M. P.'s or "the gentry," rising or declining, who bore the brunt of the civil war. It would also be interesting to have studies of those who fought for the King. But I suspect that in the Royalist areas the traditional "feudal" machinery still worked, landlords brought out their tenants, the militia was officered by the gentry of the county. The New Model was an army of a new type.

(vi) On the gentry, let us admit that we still do not know enough. I personally believe that the contemporary analyses of Winstanley, Harrington, Hobbes, Baxter, and Clarendon are still the safest guides, and that Professor Tawney is more right than Professor Trevor-Roper. But we should stop generalizing about "the gentry." Professor Trevor-Roper himself points out the regional differences which made a gentleman with £150 a year in Devon comparable with one who had far more in the home counties. We also need to know more about different types of estate management and leasing policies, about investments in trade and industry, before we can begin to see the way in which the rise of capitalism was dividing the gentry into different economic classes. We need more studies of individual families like Dr. M. Finch's admirable *The Wealth of Five North-amptonshire Families 1540–1640;* more documents like those of the Herbert and Percy families edited respectively by Dr. Kerridge and Mr. James. We also need more regional inquiries like those of Professor Dodd and Messrs. Everitt and Pennington and Roots, and local documents like the minute-book of Bedford Corporation. Such local studies will divert us from exclusive attention to the small group of men at Westminster, and help us to see the deeper social currents on which the politicians were floating.

(vii) Professor Trevor-Roper has done a great service in drawing our attention to the significance of control of the state. But this was not important merely as a source of spoils, of windfall wealth for individuals. The state was an instrument of economic power, maintaining monopolists and customs farmers, fining enclosers, endanger-

ing property by arbitrary taxation; in different hands the same instrument was used to confiscate and sell land, to pass the navigation Act which challenged the Dutch to fight for the trade of the world, to conquer Ireland and grab Spanish colonies. Yet the relation of individuals and groups to the state power still needs fuller investigation.

(viii) We also need far more understanding of ideas, especially at the point where they interact with economics. Over twenty years ago [*Economic History Review*, VI, No. 1] Mr. Wagner wrote a fascinating article on "Coke and the Rise of Economic Liberalism." This line of thought needs fuller working out; it may prove as important as that summarized in Professor Tawney's *Religion and the Rise of Capitalism*. Contemporaries were influenced by legal theories little less than by religion: Lilburne held the Bible in one hand, Coke in the other. It is therefore important to take legal history out of the hands of the lawyers, as religious history has been taken away from the theologians, and relate both to social development. Law deals with property relations, and liberty and property were the two things most strongly and consistently emphasized in the Long Parliament of 1640–1. The fact that after 1640 (and after 1660) Sir Edward Coke was regarded as *the* legal authority, whereas before 1640 his writings were suppressed by the government, shows the importance of clarity about the exact relation of his legal doctrine to the social and economic changes of the seventeenth century.

(ix) Finally, questions of religion and church government should not be "left behind the door." We must have a better explanation of their importance for contemporaries than the theory that Puritanism helps landowners to balance their income and expenditure, or encourages the bourgeoisie to grind the faces of the poor. Professor Haller has shown us how the Puritan ministers acted as organizers of something approaching a political party; and the ministers were more interested in religion than in economics. Puritanism means Vane and

Milton and Bunyan as well as Alderman Fowke, who was "not much noted for religion, but a countenancer of good ministers" and who was "deeply engaged in Bishops' lands." We are in no danger today of forgetting Alderman Fowke and his like; we are in more danger of forgetting those who fought well because they thought they were fighting God's battles. We must remember too the vision of Bacon and George Hakewill and John Preston, of a freer humanity glorifying God by abolishing evil through profounder knowledge of the world in which men live. Bacon's influence in inspiring revolt against the past became widespread only after the political revolution of the sixteen-forties: modern science entered Oxford behind the New Model Army. The connections of religion, science, politics, and economics are infinite and infinitely subtle. Religion was the idiom in which the men of the seventeenth century thought. One does not need to accept the idiom, or to take it at its face value, to see that it cannot be ignored or rejected as a simple reflex of economic needs. Any adequate interpretation of the English Revolution must give full place to questions of religion and church government, must help us to grasp the political and social implications of theological heresy.

One easy refuge is to say that it is all so complex that no interpretation at all is possible. The historian can only record the multifarious things that happened, but must not attempt to make sense of them. I believe this is to abdicate the historian's function. We need not accept Professor Trevor-Roper's interpretation to applaud his attempt to interpret. "In humane studies there are times when a new error is more life-giving than an old truth, a fertile error than a sterile accuracy." Certain things we can say. "The Puritan Revolution" failed. The City on a Hill was not built in England; the prelates came back in 1660, welcomed by many who had attacked them in 1640. The economic and political revolution succeeded to a much greater extent.

The end of the prerogative courts and of arbitrary taxation threatening security of property; sovereignty of Parliament and common law; the habit of continuous parliamentary government; effective rule of J. P.'s and town corporations uncontrolled by Star Chamber or major-generals; end of monopolies; abolition of feudal tenures, but no security for copyholders; conquest of Ireland; the Navigation Act and use of sea power for an imperialist policy — these were the lasting achievements of the years 1640–60, though some were not finally confirmed until 1688. There was much continuity of policy from the 'fifties to the 'sixties, and of administrative personnel.

But, whilst recognizing these facts, I at any rate should not wish to interpret them in crudely economic terms. Pym and the "Presbyterians" were not a mere gang of capitalists, any more than the "Independents" were a rabble of bankrupt gentlemen. And if we are to put it at its lowest, one could argue that to create the conditions for free capitalist development in England then did open up wide vistas for increasing production, for a Baconian relief of man's estate; whereas the regime of Laud and Charles I offered only a Spanish stagnation.

But my whole argument has been that we should not think *merely* in economic terms. The establishment of parliamentary supremacy, of the rule of law, no doubt mainly benefited the men of property. But on any showing the abolition of Star Chamber and High Commission and monopolies were to the advantage of the majority of Englishmen. And political ideas had outstripped constitutional achievement. The course of the Revolution itself led to the emergence of systematic democratic political theories, for the first time in modern history. The theories of Vane, Milton, the Levellers, were not whispered in a corner; they had roused large numbers of men and women to political action. They were no more forgotten than was the public execution of a King of England in the name of his people. James II did not need reminding that he had a joint in his neck.

What we need today, I suggest, is a return to contemporary interpretations, integrated with the results of recent research into industrial history and modern studies of the relation between Puritanism and the rise of capitalism. Above all, we must widen our view so as to embrace the total activity of society. Any event so complex as a revolution must be seen as a whole. Large numbers of men and women were drawn into political activity by religious and political ideals as well as by economic necessities. This sense of the largeness of the issues, and some of my criticisms of current historical fashions, were expressed by no less a person than Oliver Cromwell when he asked:

What are all our histories and other traditions of actions in former times but God manifesting Himself that he hath shaken and tumbled and trampled upon everything that He hath not planted? . . . Let men take heed and be twice advised, how they call His revolutions, the things of God and His working of things from one period to another, how, I say, they call them necessities of men's creations.

We cannot all share Cromwell's intimate knowledge of the ways of the Almighty; but we can, I hope, agree with him that mighty revolutions should not be dismissed as the unfortunate mistakes of incompetent politicians, or as the product of the skill and greed of a few cunning men. No explanation of the English Revolution will do which starts by assuming that the people who made it were knaves or fools, puppets or automata.

SUGGESTIONS FOR ADDITIONAL READING

(Unless otherwise stated, the place of publication is London.)

The seventeenth-century commentators are still worth reading in full, for although contemporaries often see only a part of the picture, and their views may be distorted by passion and prejudice, they do not necessarily see less than the modern historian, the slave of his documents. The standard scholarly edition of Edward Hyde, Earl of Clarendon, *The History of the Great Rebellion,* is that of W. D. Macray, Oxford, 1888, in six volumes; but *Selections,* ed. G. Huehns, are in "World's Classics," 1955. Light is thrown on the compilation of the book by Charles H. Firth, "Clarendon's History of the Rebellion," *English Historical Review,* XIX (1904), 26–54, 246–62, 464–83. Lucy Hutchinson, *Memoirs of the Life of Colonel Hutchinson,* ed. Charles H. Firth, 2 vols., 1885, is also in "Everyman's Library," as is Richard Baxter, *Autobiography . . . ,* ed. J. M. Lloyd-Thomas. Thomas Hobbes, *Behemoth: the History of the Causes of the Civil Wars in England, and of the counsels and artifices by which they were carried on . . . ,* is in *The English Works of Thomas Hobbes,* ed. William Molesworth, VI, 165–418, published in 1840.

Of nineteenth-century histories, probably no more than four are still worth reading. Henry Hallam, *The Constitutional History of England from the Accession of Henry VII to the Death of George II,* 1827, has four long chapters on our period; their tone is so judicious, though on the whole parliamentarian, that Macaulay wrote a violent review in *The Edinburgh Review,* September, 1828, in the attempt to establish a harsher view of Charles I and a more complete vindication of the Long Parliament. When he came to write his *History of England from the Accession of James II,* of which most of the first chapter of Vol. I (1848) is devoted to our subject, he moderated his tone but did not change his point of view; there is a convenient edition in "Everyman's Library." Leopold von Ranke was the most distinguished European historian ever to approach the history of this period in England; his *History of England, principally in the Sev-*enteenth Century, was published in German between 1859 and 1868, while the English translation is in 6 vols., Oxford, 1875. The most detailed narrative of the whole period is Samuel Rawson Gardiner, *History of England from the Accession of James I to the Outbreak of the Civil War,* 10 vols., 1883–4, after separate volumes had been issued since 1863. A hostile criticism of his methods and generalizations is Roland G. Usher, *A Critical Study of the Historical Method of Samuel Rawson Gardiner,* St. Louis, Mo., 1915.

Modern narratives may be found in Godfrey Davies, *The Early Stuarts, 1603–1660,* 2nd ed., Oxford, 1959, with the most recent bibliography; in George M. Trevelyan, *England under the Stuarts,* 3rd ed., 1946, first written in 1904, more colorful and more completely parliamentarian in sympathy; in Joseph R. Tanner, *Constitutional Conflicts of the Seventeenth Century,* Cambridge, 1928, traditional in approach but packed with quotations; in David L. Keir, *Constitutional History of Modern Britain,* 1938, remarkably balanced, and willing to admit what a weight of precedent was on the royal side; and in Cicely V. Wedgwood, *The King's Peace,* 1955, and *The King's War,* 1958, which have already been sufficiently discussed. Allen P. French, *Charles I and the Puritan Upheaval,* 1955, has some interesting chapters based on the State Papers, but is one-sided, because an attempt to explain the Puritan migration to the New World rather than a full history. Maurice P. Ashley, *England in the Seventeenth Century,* 1952, in "The Pelican History of England," is unfortunately the weakest in that series. The Marxist view is [John E. C.] Christopher Hill, *The English Revolution, 1640,* 1955, first published in 1940. The royalist case is in Esmé Wingfield-Stratford, *Charles King of England, 1600–1637,* and *King Charles and King Pym, 1637–1643,* both 1949. The relevant collections of documents are George W. Prothero, *Select Statutes and Constitutional Documents Illustrative of the Reigns of Elizabeth and*

James I, Oxford, 1894 and later eds.; Joseph R. Tanner, *Constitutional Documents of the Reign of James I*, Cambridge, 1930; and Samuel R. Gardiner, *The Constitutional Documents of the Puritan Revolution, 1625–1660*, Oxford, 1889 and later editions.

The books thus far mentioned are political or constitutional in emphasis. With social interpretations so prominent, it is important to read in full the polemical works, but also to study some of the more straightforward accounts of English economic development and social structure. A good summary is the relevant section of George N. Clark, *The Wealth of England from 1496 to 1760*, 1946. For reference there is Ephraim Lipson, *Economic History of England*, II and III, 3rd ed., 1943. Arthur P. Newton, *The Colonising Activities of the English Puritans: the Last Phase of the Elizabethan Struggle with Spain*, New Haven, Conn., 1914, is very detailed; one prominent Puritan career is described in W. Frank Craven, "The Earl of Warwick, a Speculator in Piracy," *Hispanic American Historical Review*, X (1930), 457–79. Interesting social histories are Wallace Notestein, *The English People on the Eve of Colonization, 1603–1630*, 1954, in the "New American Nation" series; and Mildred L. Campbell, *The English Yeoman under Elizabeth and the Early Stuarts*, New Haven, Conn., 1942, which has much on the contemporary attitude to social rank. More difficult to read are three books by David Mathew, *The Jacobean Age*, 1938, *The Social Structure in Caroline England*, Oxford, 1948 (esp. the chapters on "The Stratification of the Gentry" and "The Emergence of a Professional Class"), and *The England of Charles I*, 1951. Interesting local studies with some emphasis on the gentry are William G. Hoskins and H. P. R. Finberg, *Devonshire Studies*, 1952 (esp. the chapter on "Estates of the Caroline Gentry"); Peter Laslett, "The Gentry of Kent in 1640," *Cambridge Historical Journal*, IX, No. 2 (1948), 148–64; and Alan M. Everitt, *The County Committee of Kent in the Civil War*, Leicester, 1957.

The controversy over the gentry has produced the following articles. Richard H. Tawney, "The Rise of the Gentry 1558–1640," *Economic History Review*, XI (1941), 1–38; "The Rise of the Gentry: a Postscript," *ibid.*, Second Series, VII (1954), 91–7; and "Harrington's Interpretation of his Age," *Proceedings of the British Academy 1941*. Lawrence Stone, "The Anatomy of the Elizabethan Aristocracy," *Economic History Review*, XVIII (1948), 1–53; and "The Elizabethan Aristocracy, a Re-Statement," *ibid.*, Second Series, IV (1952), 302–21. Hugh R. Trevor-Roper, "The Elizabethan Aristocracy, An Anatomy Anatomized," *ibid.*, III (1951), 279–98; "The Gentry, 1540–1640," *Economic History Review Supplements*, I, 1953; "The Country House Radicals" and "The Social Causes of the Great Rebellion," both in *Historical Essays*, 1957; and "Oliver Cromwell and his Parliaments," in *Essays Presented to Sir Lewis Namier*, ed. Richard Pares and A. J. P. Taylor, 1956. J. P. Cooper, "The Counting of Manors," *Economic History Review*, Second Series, VIII (1956), 377–89, supports Trevor-Roper; Christopher Hill, "Recent Interpretations of the Civil War," in his *Puritanism and Revolution*, 1958, criticizes him. J. H. Hexter's "Storm over the Gentry" is in *Encounter*, May, 1958; rather similar conclusions are arrived at independently by Perez Zagorin in his article "The Social Interpretation of the English Revolution," *Journal of Economic History*, XIX (1959), 376–401. Attempts at analysis of the House of Commons, which may throw light on the social interpretations, are Douglas Brunton and D. H. Pennington, *Members of the Long Parliament*, 1954 (note the criticisms by B. Manning in *Past and Present*, No. 5 (May, 1954) and by Hill in "Recent Interpretations"); and Mary F. Keeler, *The Long Parliament 1640–1641: A Biographical Study of its Members*, Philadelphia, 1954, which emphasizes the members' long experience in public service.

The development of the Church of England may be followed in several monographs. Roland G. Usher, *The Reconstruction of the English Church*, 2 vols., New York, 1910, is about Bancroft's work, to which it is highly favorable. The situation which was being reformed is described, from the inside, in William P. M. Kennedy, *Elizabethan Episcopal Administra-*

tion, 3 vols. (documents with a long introduction), 1924; and from the Roman Catholic standpoint, though with wide learning, in Philip Hughes, *The Reformation in England*, III, 1954. These can be followed up by Paul A. Welsby, *Lancelot Andrewes*, 1958; by Hugh Trevor-Roper, *Archbishop Laud*, 1940 (very detailed, and note especially the chapter "Canterbury"); and by chapter VII of Mathew, *Age of Charles I*, which is penetrating on Laud. Gordon Albion, *Charles I and the Court of Rome*, 1935, shows how unfounded were suspicions of a conspiracy: such negotiations as occurred were always at cross-purposes. On Puritanism, see M. M. Knappen, *Tudor Puritanism: a Chapter in the History of Idealism*, Chicago, 1939; William Haller, *The Rise of Puritanism*, New York, 1938, and *Liberty and Reformation in the Puritan Revolution*, New York, 1955. How closely ecclesiastical affairs were entangled with social and political can be seen in Godfrey Davies, "English Political Sermons, 1603–1640," *Huntington Library Quarterly*, III (1939), 1–23 (stressing the government's appreciation of the importance of controlling the most important channel of news and opinion); in Ethyn W. Kirby, "Sermons before the Commons," *American Historical Review*, XLIV (1938–9), 528–48; and above all in Christopher Hill, *Economic Problems of the Church: from Archbishop Whitgift to the Long Parliament*, Oxford, 1956. Useful background books, not specifically about England, are John T. McNeill, *The History and Character of Calvinism*, New York, 1954; A. W. Harrison, *The Beginnings of Arminianism*, 1926; and the volume in the present series, ed. Robert Green, *Calvinism and Capitalism*.

In addition to Margaret A. Judson, *The Crisis of the Constitution: An Essay on Constitutional and Political Thought in England, 1603–45*, New Brunswick, N. J., 1949 (which has a full bibliography of printed and unpublished diaries covering parliamentary debates), the following may be consulted: John W. Allen, *English Political Thought, 1603–1660*, I, 1938; Charles H. McIlwain, *The High Court of Parliament and Its Supremacy*, New Haven, Conn., 1910, and *Constitutionalism Ancient and Modern*, Ithaca, N. Y., 1947;

Francis D. Wormuth, *The Royal Prerogative, 1603–1649*, Ithaca, 1939; Faith Thompson, *Magna Carta, Its Role in the Making of the English Constitution, 1300–1629*, Minneapolis, 1948; John G. A. Pocock, *The Ancient Constitution and the Feudal Law*, Cambridge, 1957; and, rather apart from all these in its argument, George L. Mosse, *The Struggle for Sovereignty in England from the Reign of Elizabeth to the Petition of Right*, East Lansing, Mich., 1950. On Coke, see William Holdsworth, *History of English Law*, V, 1st ed., 1924; Catherine D. Bowen, *The Lion and the Throne*, 1957, is interesting on Coke's career and conveys the atmosphere of the period, but adds nothing on the legal technicalities. The famous John N. Figgis, *The Divine Right of Kings*, Cambridge, 1896, is less useful than one would expect; it is far better to read Charles H. McIlwain, ed., *Political Works of James I*, Cambridge, Mass., 1918, both the admirable introduction and such a work as "The Trew Law of Free Monarchies"; McIlwain shows how much James' theories were developed in answer to those of the Jesuits.

It cannot be too much emphasized that a study of practical government and politics should begin with the reign of Elizabeth. Our understanding of that period has been greatly advanced by the work of John E. Neale: *The Elizabethan House of Commons*, 1949, and *Elizabeth I and Her Parliaments*, 2 vols., 1953, 1957. His *Essays in Elizabethan History*, 1958, includes the view that by 1603 the political system was on the verge of breakdown, and that only exceptional leadership could have kept it going in its Tudor form, or directed a peaceful transition to something different. The workings of royal government can be followed in David H. Willson, *King James VI and I*, 1956 (and this is also excellent on James' early Scottish experiences), and the same author's *Privy Councillors in the House of Commons, 1606–1629*, Minneapolis, 1940; Cicely V. Wedgwood, *Strafford*, 1935 (favorable to Strafford, and good on Ireland; but that subject has now been discussed at a new level of lucidity by Hugh F. Kearney, *Strafford in Ireland, 1633–41, A Study in Absolutism*, Manchester, 1959); Trevor-Roper, *Laud*; Rachel R. Reid,

The King's Council in the North, 1921; R. W. K. Hinton, "Government and Liberty under James I," *Cambridge Historical Journal,* XI, No. 1 (1953), 48–64, and "The Decline of Parliamentary Government under Elizabeth and the Early Stuarts," *ibid.,* XIII (1957), 116–32 (interesting facts and some extreme generalizations); Charles R. Mayes, "The Sale of Peerages in Early Stuart England," *Journal of Modern History,* XXIX (1957), 21–37; G. E. Aylmer, "Attempts at Administrative Reform, 1625–40," *English Historical Review,* LXXII (1957), 229–59, and "Office-Holding as a Factor in English History, 1625–42," *History,* XLIV (1959), 228–40. For government finance, see Frederick C. Dietz, *English Public Finance, 1558–1641,* New York, 1932; R. Ashton, "Deficit Finance in the Reign of James I," *Economic History Review,* Second Series, X (1957), 15–29; and, most useful of all, on the difficulties of imposing economies under James I, Richard H. Tawney, *Business and Politics under James I: Lionel Cranfield as Merchant and Minister,* Cambridge, 1958, which also has a brilliant account of English trade. For local government, an admirable study is William B. Willcox, *Gloucestershire: A Study in Local Government 1590–1640,* New Haven, 1940. On parliamentary elections, see the following articles in *English Historical Review:* R. N. Kershaw, "The Elections for the Long Parliament," XXXVIII (1923); Edith Farnham, "The Somerset Election of 1614," XLVI (1931); Mary E. Bohannon, "The Essex Election of 1604," XLVIII (1933); and Violet A. Rowe, "The Influence of the Earls of Pembroke on Parliamentary Elections 1625–41," L (1935). The activities of the House of Commons can be seen in Harold Hulme, *The Life of Sir John Eliot,* 1957 (with the fullest modern account of the 1628–9 Parliament); in Wallace Notestein, "The Winning of the Initiative by the House of Commons," *Proceedings of the British Academy 1924;* in Frances H. Relf, *The Petition of Right,* Minneapolis, 1917, and E. R. Adair, "The Petition of Right," *History,* V (1920–1), 99–103; in Willson H. Coates, "Some Observations on the Grand Remonstrance," *Journal of Modern History,* IV (1932), 1–17 (empha-

sizing how early in the Long Parliament radical claims were put forward); in Sidney R. Brett, *John Pym 1583–1643: The Statesman of the Puritan Revolution,* 1940, and in J. H. Hexter, *The Reign of King Pym,* Cambridge, Mass., 1941 (of which the greater part, however, deals with 1642–3). The recent book by Williams M. Mitchell, *The Rise of the Revolutionary Party in the English House of Commons 1603–1629,* New York, 1957, does not justify its title: it is no more than a statistical analysis of Commons leadership — who made most speeches, and sat on and reported from most committees, and how much continuity of leadership there was from parliament to parliament — and as such is interesting. To all these may be added three other biographies: John A. R. Marriott, *The Life and Times of Lucius Cary, Viscount Falkland,* 1907; Brian H. G. Wormald, *Clarendon: Politics, History, and Religion,* Cambridge, 1951; and Ethyn W. Kirby, *William Prynne: A Study in Puritanism,* Cambridge, Mass., 1931.

Most local studies concentrate upon the events of the Civil War. The following have a few interesting pages on political leadership and on divisions among the gentry: Mary Coate, *Cornwall in the Civil War and Interregnum,* Oxford, 1933; Alfred C. Wood, *Nottinghamshire in the Civil War,* Oxford, 1937; Arthur H. Dodd, *Studies in Stuart Wales,* Cardiff, 1952; and Donald H. Pennington and I. A. Roots, *The Committee at Stafford,* Manchester, 1957. Local religious conflicts are emphasized in G. H. Tupling, "The Causes of the Civil War in Lancashire," *Transactions of the Lancashire and Cheshire Antiquarian Society,* LXV (1955).

Overseas influences on the events leading to the Civil War are to some extent recognized in all the books, though outstandingly, as one might expect, in Ranke. On anti-Spanish feeling, see Louis B. Wright, "Propaganda against James I's Appeasement of Spain," *Huntington Library Quarterly,* VI (1943), 149–72. On Irish influences, J. R. MacCormack, "The Irish Adventurers and the English Civil War," *Irish Historical Studies,* X (1956–7), 21–58 (on gentry and City land speculators); and Thomas L. Coonan, *The Irish Catholic Confederacy and the Puritan Revolution,* Dublin, 1954 (outstandingly hostile to the English Parliament). For the European background in general, consult David Ogg, *Europe in the Seventeenth Century,* 4th ed., 1943, and Cicely V. Wedgwood, *The Thirty Years' War,* 1938. For the rise of Absolutism, see George N. Clark, *The Seventeenth Century,* Oxford, 1929 (esp. chapter V, "Comparative Constitutional History"); Cicely V. Wedgwood, *Riche-*

lieu and the French Monarchy, 1949; and F. L. Carsten, *The Origins of Prussia,* Oxford, 1954, and *Princes and Parliaments in Germany,* Oxford, 1959.

Finally, in a category by itself, is the analysis of the development of revolutions, with the author's expert knowledge of the French Revolution as the base, [Clarence] Crane Brinton, *The Anatomy of Revolution,* rev. ed., 1953: it is most stimulating.